PENGUIN BOOKS

The CSIRO Wellbeing Plan for Kids

About the Authors

Dr Jane Bowen is a research dietitian and contributing author of the *CSIRO Total Wellbeing Diet* series as well as mum to Ava. She has conducted clinical nutritional trials to establish the health potential of diets, foods and nutrients. Jane coordinated the 2007 Australian Children's National Nutrition and Physical Activity Survey.

Dr Nadia Corsini is a research psychologist with a passion for children's health and wellbeing. She has recently designed and implemented strategies to help parents 'train the tastebuds' and encourage vegetable consumption in their preschoolers.

Claire Gardner has both dietetics and physical-activity qualifications and a strong background in public health nutrition. She has been involved in a variety of state and national health initiatives promoting a healthy lifestyle. She is mum to young son Harry.

Dr Rebecca Golley is a paediatric research dietitian who has worked with over 500 parents and children. Her research has focused on developing practical information and resources for parents to help them inspire their families to lead a healthy lifestyle.

Dr Amy Slater is a research psychologist, registered psychologist and mum to Lily and Lachlan. She has worked clinically with parents and children who have a wide range of developmental and behavioural issues. Her research has focused on adolescent sport participation, media use and body-image concerns.

The Commonwealth Scientific and Industrial Research Organisation (CSIRO), Australia's national science agency, ranks in the top one per cent of the world scientific institutions in 12 out of 22 research fields. CSIRO Human Nutrition conducts research into human health, including disease prevention, management and effective treatment.

Foreword by
Dr Manny Noakes

the CSIRO
wellbeing plan for
kids

PENGUIN BOOKS

Published by the Penguin Group
Penguin Group (Australia)
250 Camberwell Road, Camberwell, Victoria 3124, Australia
(a division of Pearson Australia Group Pty Ltd)
Penguin Group (USA) Inc.
375 Hudson Street, New York, New York 10014, USA
Penguin Group (Canada)
90 Eglinton Avenue East, Suite 700, Toronto, Canada ON M4P 2Y3
(a division of Pearson Penguin Canada Inc.)
Penguin Books Ltd
80 Strand, London WC2R 0RL England
Penguin Ireland
25 St Stephen's Green, Dublin 2, Ireland
(a division of Penguin Books Ltd)
Penguin Books India Pvt Ltd
11 Community Centre, Panchsheel Park, New Delhi – 110 017, India
Penguin Group (NZ)
67 Apollo Drive, Rosedale, North Shore 0632, New Zealand
(a division of Pearson New Zealand Ltd)
Penguin Books (South Africa) (Pty) Ltd
24 Sturdee Avenue, Rosebank, Johannesburg 2196, South Africa

Penguin Books Ltd, Registered Offices: 80 Strand, London, WC2R 0RL, England

First published by Penguin Group (Australia), 2009

10 9 8 7 6 5 4 3 2 1

Design by Nikki Townsend and Megan Pigott © Penguin Group (Australia)
Photographs on back cover (second from left and far right) and pp 114–20, 124–39,
142–51, 156–253 and 257–65 by Rob Palmer; on back cover (second from right), spine,
and pp ii–x, 4, 6, 8, 9, 10, 14, 17, 25, 28 (top left), 32, 33, 37 (bottom), 44, 49, 74, 84, 88,
105 and 110 by Nicholas Wilson; on pp 1, 2, 3, 23, 27, 28–9, 30, 35, 37 (top), 63, 70 and
254 by Richard Birch; on pp 26–7, 42, 46, 48, 50, 52–3, 57, 58–9, 64, 65, 71, 72, 76–7, 78,
80, 83, 90–1, 99, 101, 104, 108–9, 112, 122, 140 and 154 by Getty Images.
Recipes by Heidi Flett
Food styling by Jane Hann
Food preparation by Jennifer Tolhurst and Tracey Meharg

Typeset in Berling by Post Pre-Press Group, Brisbane, Queensland
Colour reproduction by Splitting Image, Clayton, Victoria
Printed and bound in China by Everbest Printing Co. Ltd

National Library of Australia
Cataloguing-in-Publication data:

        The CSIRO wellbeing plan for kids.

        Includes index.
        Bibliography.
        ISBN 9780143008743

        Children – Health and hygiene – Australia.
        Children – Australia – Nutrition.
        Health promotion – Australia.
        Cookery.
        Physical fitness for children.

        613.2083

penguin.com.au

Speak with your doctor if you have concerns about any aspects
of your child's health, or an Accredited Practicing Dietitian (APD)
if you are thinking of making significant changes to your child's
diet. Parenting helplines are also available in each state to provide
information, counselling and support for parents and carers of
children. Visit the Raising Children Network: the Australian
parenting website raisingchildren.net.au

Go to our website at csiro.au/science/WellbeingPlanForKids for
further resources and links on children and family health and
wellbeing. Our website also provides a way for you to tell us
your thoughts about this book.

Contents

Acknowledgements

We would like to acknowledge the following people whose feedback on our manuscript has assisted us in improving the readability, accuracy and relevance of the messages and advice for our readers: Associate Professor Tony Okely, Faculty of Education and Child Obesity Research Centre, University of Wollongong; Dr Leah Brennan, Clinical and Health Psychologist and Senior Research Fellow, Parenting Research Centre; Professor Louise Baur, Discipline of Paediatrics & Child Health, Sydney Medical School, University of Sydney; Associate Professor Clare Collins, Fellow of the Dietitians Association of Australia, School of Health Sciences, University of Newcastle; Professor Marika Tiggemann, School of Psychology, Flinders University; Dr Michael Gradisar, School of Psychology, Flinders University; Professor Peter Clifton, CSIRO Human Nutrition; the Department of Health and Ageing, Canberra; and the numerous researchers and colleagues who provided advice on specific topics.

At CSIRO, thanks to Gilly Hendrie and Peta Newbold for contributing to the manuscript, and to Belinda Wyld, Peter Royle, Kaylene Pickering and Vanessa Courage for field-testing our ideas and recipes.

We would like to thank Associate Professor Manny Noakes, Dr Phil Mohr, Professor Carlene Wilson and Dr Grant Brinkworth for their ongoing guidance, support and faith in this book.

A big thank you to the recipe and photography team, in particular Heidi Flett for her inspiring recipes. And to the team at Penguin – Julie Gibbs, Ingrid Ohlsson, Jane Morrow, Claire de Medici, Nikki Townsend, Megan Pigott and Elena Cementon – for their professional guidance and for transforming the manuscript into an attractive and practical resource for parents.

Foreword

Dr Manny Noakes

Most of us would agree that eating well, being active and having a positive body image are important for our children's current and future health and wellbeing. But how we prioritise and achieve this with today's busy lifestyle is a significant challenge.

As researchers we have learned a lot from how our previous publications have been helpful to many Australians. In particular, the *CSIRO Total Wellbeing Diet* books have been practical and effective guides to healthy weight management. So much so that we have received many wonderful emails telling us how these books have transformed people's lives.

In order to better understand what aspects of these publications were most helpful, we commissioned a consumer study. What we found was intriguing. Firstly, we know that over 60 per cent of Australians are aware of the CSIRO Total Wellbeing Diet and an estimated 540 000 people have lost an average of 6 kg using this plan. We found that older individuals tended to use the meal plans more often and that younger people used the recipe and general information more regularly. It appeared that younger groups had a preference for a very flexible approach to changing lifestyle habits.

With this information in mind, we wanted to ensure that in a publication aimed at families with children we were providing information that was both relevant and practical. This book differs from our previous publications. It is not focused on weight loss and it is not a diet for children. Although we know that approximately 25 per cent of children are overweight or obese, this publication is for all Australian families with children. We hope that the useful tips and strategies contained here inspire and help parents and caregivers to make their family's lifestyle a top priority. Making even small changes can lead to long-lasting health benefits for the entire family. The emphasis is very much on how to achieve this.

The talented team that has put this book together has worked tirelessly to assemble the best available scientific advice in a way that is easy to follow and gently guides us into habits for healthy living. The team understands the importance of advice that is both motivating and achievable despite the challenges of juggling work and family life.

For further resources as well as links on children and family health and wellbeing, go to our website at csiro.au/science/WellbeingPlanForKids. Our website also provides a way for you to tell us your thoughts about this book.

I trust you will enjoy this book and gain useful knowledge and skills to benefit the health and wellbeing of your family.

Associate Professor Manny Noakes is the stream leader for the Diet and Lifestyle program at CSIRO Human Nutrition, a multidisciplinary team of nutritionists, psychologists and exercise physiologists engaged in developing innovative programs for improving healthy lifestyle behaviour among Australians. She also manages clinical trials that provide scientific evidence for the efficacy of diet and exercise programs on health. Manny has published over 100 scientific papers, with a major emphasis on diet composition, weight loss and cardiovascular health. She is a senior lecturer in the School of Medicine at Flinders University, affiliate senior lecturer in the Department of Obstetrics and Gynaecology at the University of Adelaide, and affiliate associate professor in the Department of Medicine at the University of Adelaide.

raising healthy, happy children

As parents we want the best for our children, for their health, education and safety – their overall wellbeing. In today's world where everyone has too much to do in next to no time, how can you know which foods, drinks and activities are best for your child – and then find the time and inspiration to make this happen?

In addition, children have their own personalities and preferences, which influence what they like to eat and do. This book is designed to help you tackle some of these challenges. It focuses on practical information you can use to positively influence your child's eating and physical activity habits.

A snapshot of Australian children's health and lifestyle

In 2007, CSIRO was involved in undertaking the first national survey of Australian children's eating and activity habits in over a decade. This important piece of research shows that most children consume enough energy and nutrients to grow and be active. However, some worrying patterns are seen when we look at the foods these nutrients are coming from. Children across all ages are not eating enough dairy foods, fruit and vegetables and wholegrain cereal foods for good health. They are also consuming too much saturated fat, sugar and salt. As children get older they are less active, sleep less and watch more television.

What do parents say?

The list of things that parents think and worry about for their children is long! Many Australian parents share our concern about what children are eating and how they spend their time. To better understand what was on the minds of parents, in 2008 we undertook a survey of over 1200 parents of 2–16-year-olds from around Australia. We asked about the issues that most concern parents, and about the factors that influence what their children eat, their physical activity patterns and sedentary behaviours. The survey showed us the following things.

- The top issue concerning Australian parents was their children's education. The second most common response was their children's health and wellbeing.
- When asked specifically about food, 46 per cent of parents reported that they are concerned about the amount of 'junk' food – fatty and sugary foods and drinks – their children eat.
- Common barriers to children eating better include children's opposition to eating 'healthy' food, the availability and low cost of unhealthy food, and the pressures of a busy lifestyle.
- Less than a third of parents were concerned about their children's level of physical activity, although this was a bigger issue for parents of older children. Many parents assume their children are active enough at school. Lack of time and unsuitable weather were the most common reasons parents gave for their children not being more active.

These unhealthy patterns have long-term implications for their future heart, metabolic and dental health as well as cancer risks.

This study also confirms that a quarter of Australian children – children of all ages, not just older children – are overweight or obese. In adults, rates of overweight and obesity are even higher and are risk factors for lifestyle diseases such as diabetes and heart disease. Avoiding unhealthy weight gain in childhood is critical to support lifelong health and wellbeing.

The results of this survey reinforce that we must ensure our children get the healthiest start to life by establishing good eating habits, enjoying an active lifestyle and maintaining a healthy weight. Prevention is better than cure!

We also asked parents what support would help achieve a healthier lifestyle for their family. Knowing *what* food and activity children need was a concern raised by some parents, but knowing *how* to encourage children to adopt healthy habits was what parents told us would really help. Parents asked for strategies and practical advice to overcome the common barriers – for example, ways to manage child resistance to healthy foods, to be active no matter what the weather and to incorporate healthy habits into increasingly busy lives.

We have listened to and heard parents' concerns. While the health and wellbeing of Australian children depends on a team effort – individuals, communities, health professionals, industry and government all working together – this book aims to help parents and families play their part.

Healthy homes, healthy families

Children spend a significant amount of their time at home. Even as outside influences – childcare, school, friends, the media – start to influence more of a child's day, the home remains central in their lives, whether they are 5 or 15.

Home, therefore, is one of the key places where children learn what to eat and how to lead an active life. Parents and caregivers are the first and most important influences on what children eat, how they get about and what they play – parents determine what food is in the fridge and pantry, what's on the menu for meals and snacks, when and what children watch on television and what activities they do in their spare time.

Less obviously, but importantly, parents' habits and values shape how children feel about eating well and being active. If children grow up in a home in which eating a wide variety of nutritious food and being active is normal, they are more likely to take these habits into adult life and pass them on to their own family one day.

How has research been used in this book?

Over the last decade, researchers have highlighted the many ways in which parents and homes can promote healthy eating and lifestyle habits for children. These can be summarised under four headings and are key themes throughout this book.

1. Be informed

In this book we get back to basics on essential information. This will help you wade through the endless food choices available and filter the mass of – often conflicting – health messages. This is covered in **Part 1: Before you begin**, and is broken up into: **Chapter 1: Supporting your child's health and wellbeing, Chapter 2: The good food essentials, Chapter 3: Leading an active lifestyle** and **Chapter 4: Ages and stages of childhood**.

2. In sight, in mind

The types of food in the pantry or fridge and the play equipment available at home will generally reflect what children eat and what activities they undertake. This works for healthy and unhealthy habits: stocking up on fruit encourages children to eat it, and keeping crisps in the cupboard will also encourage them to be consumed. Similarly, having a bat and ball handy

will tempt children to play backyard cricket, while having a television in their bedroom encourages them to spend more time in front of it. A supportive home environment helps the healthy choice be the easy choice for children. Looking at what's in the kitchen, how you can encourage the consumption of healthy foods, and the opportunities for children to be active are covered in **Chapter 3: Leading and active lifestyle** and **Chapter 6: Making good food available at home**.

3. Be a proactive parent

As parents we influence our children's habits by the words of encouragement or feedback we offer, the expectations and boundaries we set and the ways we reward or reinforce behaviour. In **Chapter 5: A parenting tool kit**, we describe key parenting skills and strategies that can be used to encourage children to eat well and be active.

4. Be a good role model

Children are sponges, soaking up information from the world around them. The habits, values and beliefs they observe at home and from their parents are where they first learn what to eat, how to be active and the value of a healthy lifestyle. If you enjoy healthy food, having fun and being active, they will too. This is so important that it is a theme repeated throughout this book!

How to use this book

This book provides information, advice, tools and resources for making eating well and being active a way of life for your family. While the information in the book uses our research knowledge and experience working with Australian families, we are mindful that every family is unique.

See the book as a starting point that can be used in a number of ways depending on what you and your family need.

Throughout the book we refer to 'your child', but if you have more than one child, the information applies to all of the children (and adults!) in your family.

In **Part 1: Before you begin**, we introduce the key information on children's growth and wellbeing, nutrition, physical activity and parenting skills. These chapters provide the facts and knowledge that can help you begin making changes to your family's lifestyle.

In **Part 2: Making changes**, we provide practical solutions to eight key lifestyle habits. We have chosen to focus on these particular habits because together they will make the biggest difference to achieving a healthy and active lifestyle. These are:

- Training tastebuds
- Keeping an eye on snacks
- Phasing out sweet drinks
- Starting the day with breakfast
- Preparing healthy lunches
- Making evening meals easier
- Reducing screen time
- Becoming an active family

For each habit we present a step-by-step guide to making improvements as a family. We begin by setting the scene and highlighting areas you may wish to change. We then ask you to set specific goals relevant to your family and provide a range of strategies to start making changes. We also provide practical solutions to make the changes easier and help manage tricky situations. You are able to modify the specific changes so they are relevant to your family, and to tackle one change at a time.

In **Part 3: Recipes**, we include more than 100 healthy, delicious recipes that are easy to prepare. They suit a wide range of situations, from 'almost instant' meals for busy nights and slow-cooked meals that can be prepared ahead of time, to healthy alternatives to takeaway and some creative ideas for breakfast and lunch.

In **Part 4: Useful tools**, we provide a shopping guide for stocking the pantry, fridge and freezer with healthy options, as well as some key cooking practices to give your regular family favourite recipes a healthy makeover.

Not a weight-loss guide

It is important to say up front that this book is not a weight-loss book. We discuss healthy weight levels for children, but our focus is on helping achieve balanced, nutritious eating habits for your whole family. The scope of the book also doesn't allow for in-depth discussion of certain age groups (for example, babies and introducing solid foods) or certain health issues common in children (for example, asthma or managing allergies).

1

before you begin

supporting your child's health and wellbeing

Your child's health and wellbeing is about more than avoiding illness. Making sure that your child eats, plays and sleeps well will help them grow and give them a great start to life.

It is natural for you to want your child to be safe, healthy and happy and to do well at school. But with so many competing demands, it can sometimes be hard to stay focused on all aspects of your child's health and wellbeing all the time.

There are four important ways you can positively influence your child's health and wellbeing.

1. Offer a variety of healthy foods.
2. Provide lots of opportunities to be active and limit entertainment screen time.
3. Encourage them to get plenty of quality sleep.
4. Help them feel confident and safe by building their self-esteem and resilience and a positive body image.

By helping your child set up lifestyle habits that support health and wellbeing from an early age, you will be giving them a great start to help them through life. This chapter focuses on children's appetite, activity, sleep and confidence.

Balancing appetite and activity

From a young age your child needs your support so they can balance a good mix of food with appropriate levels of physical activity, to maintain a healthy weight for them and stay healthy on the inside. The amount and quality of food your child needs depends on their gender, age, growth and activity level. In **Chapter 2: The good food essentials** we include a guide to the appropriate amount and type of food for children at different ages, and **Chapter 3: Leading an active lifestyle** talks more about physical activity.

Appetite

The body is generally good at signalling when we are hungry or full. But in today's world of tasty, convenient foods, the tendency to listen to these signals can be lost. Help your child stay tuned in to their hunger and fullness signals by:

- providing appropriate portion sizes (the size of a meal or drink is one of the biggest influences of how much a child eats)
- offering nutritious foods (high-kilojoule foods and drinks that pack a lot of kilojoules into small portions are easy to overeat)
- sticking to a meal and snack routine (passive eating – such as eating in front of the television – or grazing makes it easy to overeat)

- keeping mealtimes relaxed (encourage your child to eat only as much as they need to feel satisfied – pushing them to eat more teaches them to override their body's signals).

The quality of the food your child eats will determine whether they get the vitamins, minerals and other nutrients they need to support their health and wellbeing. Foods and drinks that are high in fat, sugar and other refined carbohydrates can make it easy to fill up on kilojoules but miss out on important nutrients. Without the right food, it is harder for your child's appetite to do its job – to tell your child when they have had enough, and when food and activity levels are balanced.

Activity

Young children naturally enjoy playing, and their playtime provides opportunities to develop movement skills, coordination and confidence – aspects that are part of an active lifestyle in both childhood and adulthood. In the same way that convenience foods encourage overeating, many popular recreation activities (such as television and game consoles) encourage too much *sitting*. So, it is important to support your child's play activities by:

- providing lots of opportunities for active play, both indoors and outdoors
- setting limits on television time and screen-based activities
- praising your child for their effort and helping them seek out physical activity they enjoy
- being active with your child.

It's what's on the inside that counts!

How your child looks from the outside is only half the story – there is also lots happening on the inside. A slim child who eats lots of unhealthy food or is not very active could be unhealthy on the inside. All children (and adults) benefit from the right balance of food and activity, regardless of their weight. Risk factors for diseases such as obesity, heart disease and diabetes can originate early in life, and some Australian children are experiencing these worrying health problems. Children can also form unhealthy lifestyle patterns that can follow them into adulthood. One way to help your child stay healthy on the inside is to ensure they have access to the right mix of healthy foods for their needs plus plenty of physical activity each day.

Sleep

Sleep is vital for your child's health and well-being. Getting enough quality sleep will help them grow, develop and learn to their full potential. Children who get enough sleep at night can function better during the day, be happier and display fewer health and behavioural problems.

How much sleep?

The amount of sleep children need varies with age and also for each individual child. As a guide, preschoolers generally need between 10 and 13 hours each night, primary-school-aged children need around 11 hours each night, and adolescents need between 8 and 10 hours each night.

To work out an appropriate bedtime for your child you might need to begin with when they need to wake up in the morning in order to get to childcare, kindergarten or school on time and then count backwards the appropriate number of hours. As your child – or teenager – becomes more independent in many aspects of life, they will still benefit from your guidance on an appropriate bedtime.

How to encourage quality sleep

The keys to getting quality sleep are a regular routine and a calm sleeping environment. Set clear, consistent boundaries about routines and the amount of sleep your child needs. This means setting a bedtime and sticking to it. Have a predictable and calm evening routine that suits your child's age; for younger children this might include giving a bedtime warning such as, 'One more puzzle and then it is time to get ready for bed,' and following through on your warning each time. Have a wind-down time; for younger children this may include reading a story, while older children may like to read to themselves or listen to relaxing music. Avoid stimulating activities such as watching television or 'wrestling'-type games. Avoid caffeinated drinks for several hours before bedtime. Your child's sleeping environment should be quiet, reasonably dark and a comfortable temperature, and should not contain distractions such as a television, computers or mobile phones.

For more about teenagers and sleep see the adolescent section of **Chapter 4: Ages and stages of childhood**, page 36.

Resilience, self-esteem and body image
Resilience

Children need to feel loved, good about themselves and confident to face life's experiences and challenges. Resilience is all about how well children cope with and bounce back from these challenges.

Build resilience in your child by:
* providing comfort when they are upset or overwhelmed
* encouraging them to talk about how they are feeling when things don't work out, and helping them to think of solutions to their problems
* developing independence by allowing them to make decisions that are appropriate for their age; for example, a preschooler could choose which of two T-shirts they will wear that day, a primary-school-aged child could choose an after-school snack from two healthy options you provide.

Self-esteem

Self-esteem is all about how your child feels about who they are. Children who feel confident and good about themselves are more likely to take a positive approach to challenges and cope better with disappointments.

Build positive self-esteem in your child by:
* showing an interest in what they are doing and learning
* providing encouragement and praise for things they have done well and also for the effort made trying something new
* telling them the ways you think they are special and unique.

Healthy body image

Children are constantly exposed to images of unrealistic body ideals on television and in movies, magazines and music videos. The discrepancy between the ideal body shape – extremely thin for women and girls and extremely muscular for men and boys – and reality leaves many children, particularly adolescents, feeling dissatisfied with their bodies, which can lead to anxiety, depression and eating disorders.

Help your child feel good about their body by:
* teaching them that bodies come in a variety of shapes and sizes – the ideal body weight for them is the weight that allows them to feel energetic and lead a healthy life
* teaching them to focus on what their body can do, rather than how it looks
* ensuring they know they are loved and valued for who they are, rather than how they look

- avoiding negative comments about weight and shape, including comments about your own weight and shape
- being aware of the messages they are being exposed to in television shows, magazines, music and toys; if you are not happy with these messages, minimise their exposure. You could ask friends and relatives not to give your child toys that promote particular messages, set boundaries about the types of television shows your child can watch and screen the magazines or music videos they are exposed to.

Keeping an eye on your child's health and wellbeing

Keeping track of your child's health and wellbeing – what they eat, their activity levels, sleep patterns and confidence levels – is important. Keeping track, or monitoring, is all about gathering evidence. Being aware of these things for your child can help motivate you for action and guide you to take the best steps for your child and family. In Part 2 of this book you will find many tools to help you keep track of eating and activity habits that influence your child's health and wellbeing.

Watching children grow

One outward sign of children's health and wellbeing is their physical growth. Growth represents changes in children's height and weight over time. You may remember having your child's growth as a baby recorded using height and weight charts. From the age of 2 (and throughout childhood and adolescence), children's height and weight is still used to keep track of their growth. However, now their height and weight is used to calculate a body mass index (BMI) which is plotted on a chart that takes into account their gender, their age and their weight relative to their height. See pages 266 and 267 for BMI charts for girls and boys 2–20 years. A child's pattern of growth – a sequence of measurements (at least two or three) – is more informative than a single measurement.

Ask your doctor or health professional to help you keep track of your child's growth on a BMI chart. When you visit your doctor with your child, their height and weight can be measured and plotted on a BMI chart. Make this a regular part of your child's health care, particularly if their growth appears to be veering up or down from their usual pattern.

BMI growth chart calculators are also available on the Internet for you to use to record your child's growth over time. A useful BMI calculator is available from the US Centers for Disease Control (CDC) website at http://apps.nccd.cdc.gov/dnpabmi/Calculator.aspx, which also helps interpret what your child's results mean.

Making sense of growth charts

Even though children come in all shapes and sizes, if children are developing normally their growth will follow a pattern. Growth charts show a number of curved lines – percentile lines – which show how boys and girls of different ages, shapes and sizes can be expected to grow.

Percentiles are not grades or scores – the 10th percentile is not a failure, nor is the 95th percentile better than the 50th percentile. The lines are simply different growth patterns for boys and girls at different ages. For example, if Grace is plotted on the 50th percentile, we would expect that for girls her age, half would be bigger than Grace and half would be smaller.

- A BMI between the 5th and 85th percentile indicates a healthy weight for most children.
- A BMI below the 5th percentile indicates a child may be underweight.
- A BMI above the 85th percentile indicates a child may be overweight.
- A BMI above the 95th percentile indicates a child may be obese.

But remember that these numbers are only a guide, especially if it is only a once-off measurement. If your child is close to the 5th or 85th percentile line, check again in a month or so as this may reflect the healthy weight for them, a recent growth spurt or inaccuracies in measuring height or weight.

Example

Katie is 14 years old, weighs 50 kg and is 1.57 m (157 cm) tall. Her BMI would therefore be:

50 divided by 1.57 squared: $50/(1.57 \times 1.57) = 20.3$

According to the growth chart on page 266, Katie sits on the 61st percentile, between the 50th and 75th percentiles. This is a healthy weight for Katie. This is supported by her growth tracking along this line throughout her childhood.

Example

Michael is 6 years old, weighs 21 kg and is 1.1 m (110 cm) tall. His BMI would therefore be:

21 divided by 1.1 squared: $21/(1.1 \times 1.1) = 17.4$

Once a child's BMI has been plotted on a growth chart, there are two things to look at: where the child is placed on the chart and whether they are moving up or down from that position over time. A child's pattern of growth – whether they stay generally along one line over time – is more important than which line your child is on at one point in time. The growth pattern will show if a child is tracking consistently along one line or is veering away from the line they have been following. A change in pattern – a shift up or down from the line your child has been following – is reason to take a closer look with the help of a health professional.

However, where a child sits on the growth chart is a guide to whether they are underweight, overweight or within a healthy weight range.

Overweight is becoming a more common concern for children today; close to 25 per cent of Australian children are overweight or obese. Overweight children are more likely than children within the healthy weight range to stay overweight into adulthood, especially without their parents' help. Without support, studies have shown that:

40 per cent of overweight **4-year-olds** become overweight adults

60 per cent of overweight **6–9-year-olds** become overweight adults

60 per cent of overweight **teenagers** become overweight adults

Excess weight in children of all ages can lead to:

- being teased, bullied or ignored by their peers
- having low self-esteem and poor body image
- feeling too self-conscious to take part in sports and games
- trying dangerous fad diets and skipping meals
- bone or joint problems, or sleep difficulties
- high blood pressure, high blood cholesterol levels, type 2 diabetes or high insulin levels, diseases of the liver and gallbladder
- an increased risk of heart disease, diabetes, respiratory disease, certain cancers, fertility problems and arthritis in adulthood.

According to the growth chart on page 267 he sits on the 88th percentile, between the 85th and 90th percentile, which indicates he may be overweight. One year ago Michael's BMI-for-age was on the 75th percentile. It has gradually been shifting upwards and signals that it is time to take a closer look at the types of food he is consuming and his activity patterns, then take action to slow or halt the increase.

What can I do?

Being underweight can be sign that children are not getting the nutrition they need to grow and develop. Being overweight can be a sign of an imbalance between how much children eat and how active they are. It is important to be aware of your child being either underweight or over-weight and to take appropriate action in either situation.

My child may be underweight

For some children it is normal to follow one of the lower lines on the growth chart. There may be a problem if your child's BMI starts to veer below the percentile line they normally follow. This is why it is important to measure their growth a few times a year. Talk to your doctor if your child is not gaining weight, has recently lost weight or has had tummy problems such as diarrhoea or vomiting.

My child may be overweight

For some children it is normal to follow one of the higher lines on the growth chart, but it can also mean they are carrying more weight than is healthy for them. It can be hard to recognise your child is overweight because we are surrounded by big adults and big children. Comparing your child to their friends may not be helpful. It is best to use the growth charts regularly. There may be a problem if your child's BMI starts to veer above the percentile line they normally follow or sits above the 85th percentile line consistently when you monitor their growth over a period of time, such as for two or three measurements over six months.

The good news is that there is a lot you can do to help your child achieve a healthy weight. Overweight is influenced by our food and activity environment and lifestyle. The information and resources in this book will give you the strategies to kick-start and stick to a healthy way of eating and living for your whole family. Your child will need support, acceptance and encouragement; do not make them feel guilty about their food choices, and do not promote dieting. Being too restrictive can deprive them of important nutrition and slow their growth.

The other good news is that your child is still growing and you can use this time to help them grow into their height by slowing down their rate of weight gain. In most cases, keeping a child's weight steady while they grow taller will be enough to get them back to a healthy BMI. For teenagers or children carrying a lot of excess weight, the safest approach may be gradual, small weight loss. Seek help from a paediatrician or health professional with expertise in child weight management.

Talking about weight

Weight can be a sensitive issue for parents and children of all ages. A negative focus on a child's weight can be damaging to their self-esteem and may lead to unhealthy eating behaviours, especially in teenagers. Focus on the things that influence weight, not weight itself, to encourage children to feel confident about their bodies:

- Be a role model for a healthy lifestyle.
- Encourage children to eat well and be active.
- Promote a positive body image by encouraging and praising what your child's body can do – for example, learning to ride a bike, catching a ball or being able to dance.
- Avoid commenting on body weight (even your weight) in front of your child.
- Avoid calling your child fat, telling them to lose weight or promoting dieting.

Related information

See **Chapter 6: Making good food available at home**, **Chapter 14: Reducing screen time** and **Chapter 15: Becoming an active family** for useful tips and step-by-step guides to help you influence your child's health and wellbeing by offering a variety of healthy foods and lots of opportunities each day to be active.

the good food essentials

Knowing which foods to offer your child is the first step towards developing healthy eating habits for the whole family.

Figuring out which foods are best for your family doesn't have to be difficult. The concept of basic food groups has been around for a long time and it is still a great tool. These food groups cover the spectrum of nutrients your child's body needs to operate at its best – for optimal growth, learning, immune function and general good health – and form the basis of your family's healthy eating plan.

Balancing energy and nutrients

Providing appropriate quantities of foods from the basic food groups will give your child the right balance of energy and nutrients. The number of serves and serving sizes of each food group children need will depend on their age and activity level. Use the table on page 19 to get familiar with the basic food groups.

What does my child need?

It is hard to say exactly how many serves of each food group children of different ages, gender, body sizes and activity levels need. The table on page 19 has the number of serves of each food group to meet lower, moderate and higher kilojoule needs.

As a general guide:

- older children, boys (particularly in adolescence), and those who are very active or having a growth spurt have higher kilojoule needs
- younger children and those who are less active have lower kilojoule needs
- toddlers and preschoolers might be satisfied with smaller serving sizes than those listed in the table – let their appetite guide how much they need to eat.

Serving sizes for young children

As a guide for toddlers and preschoolers, one serve of vegetables or fruit might be equal to their age in tablespoons. For example, if they are 3 years old, a serve of vegetables is 3 tablespoons. Use the palm of their hand as a guide to a suitable serving size for meat and alternatives, and the size of their fist for a serving of bread and cereals. Thinking of serving sizes in this way for young children (up to around 5 years) means the portions will gradually increase as they get older.

Wholegrain breads and cereals

Aim for 4–8 serves a day and make at least half of these wholegrain varieties.

1 serve =
- 1 slice bread
- 1 medium roll, 1 crumpet or 1 English muffin
- ½ cup cooked rice, pasta, noodles or couscous
- ½ cup cooked porridge
- ¾ cup high-fibre breakfast cereal (such as Weeties or Mini-Wheats)
- 2 Weet-Bix or Vita Brits
- ¼ cup untoasted muesli or oats

Why does my child need wholegrain breads and cereals?

Wholegrain foods contain more vitamins and fibre than refined 'white' bread, rice and pasta – and they are more filling. Wholegrain foods are also digested more slowly than 'white' foods, which means that the glucose – the main fuel for muscles and the brain – is released over a longer period of time.

Wholegrain foods include mixed grain, wholemeal and rye breads, rolls and dry biscuits, brown rice, wholemeal pasta, wholemeal crumpets and English muffins, oats, porridge, muesli and wholegrain breakfast cereals. Cereal products (such as pasta, white rice and couscous) and refined breads can still be a part of a healthy eating plan, but balance them with wholegrain foods.

Fruit and vegetables

Aim for 2–3 serves of fruit and 4–5 serves of vegetables a day.

1 serve fruit =
- 1 medium apple, pear, orange, peach or banana
- 2 apricots, kiwi fruit or plums
- 1 cup canned fruit pieces
- 1½ tablespoons dried fruit
- ½ cup (125 ml) fruit juice

1 serve vegetables =
- ½ cup cooked vegetables or legumes (lentils, chickpeas, baked beans)
- 1 medium potato (about 150 g)
- 1 cup salad such as green/garden salad, tabouleh or coleslaw

Basic food groups

	1 serve equals	Lower kilojoule needs (4–8 yrs)	Moderate kilojoule needs (9–13 yrs)	Higher kilojoule needs (14–18 yrs)*
Wholegrain breads and cereals	1 slice bread 1 medium roll 1 crumpet 1 English muffin ½ cup cooked rice, pasta, noodles or couscous ½ cup cooked porridge ¾ cup high-fibre breakfast cereal 2 Weet-Bix ¼ cup untoasted muesli or oats	4	6	8
Fruit	1 medium piece of fruit 2 small pieces of fruit 1 cup canned fruit pieces 1½ tablespoons dried fruit ½ cup (125 ml) fruit juice	2	2	3
Vegetables	½ cup cooked vegetables or legumes 1 medium potato 1 cup salad	4	5	5
Lean meat, poultry, fish and legumes	65–100 g cooked meat (beef, veal, lamb, chicken or pork) ½ cup (85 g) cooked lean mince 80–120 g cooked fish 2 eggs ½ cup cooked legumes	1	1.5	1.5
Fat-reduced dairy foods	1 cup fat-reduced milk or calcium-enriched dairy alternative 200 g fat-reduced yoghurt 40 g fat-reduced cheese 1 cup fat-reduced custard	2	3	3
Oils, nuts and seeds	1 teaspoon oil 1 teaspoon margarine 1 tablespoon nuts/seeds 1 tablespoon avocado 1 teaspoon nut paste 2 teaspoons mayonnaise	6	6	8

* Age brackets provided are a guide only. See pages 17–18 for information on choosing the best kilojoule needs for your child's age, sex and activity level.

> ### What does Glycemic Index mean?
> Glycemic Index (GI) is a number given to foods that contain carbohydrate. It describes how quickly (a high number) or slowly (a low number) the carbohydrate is broken down to glucose. High-GI foods contain carbohydrates that are digested quickly; low-GI foods are preferable because they give a gradual, long-lasting release of glucose. One easy way to choose low-GI breads and cereals is to look for wholegrain options. Visit glycemicindex.com for more information.

Why does my child need fruit and vegetables?

As well as bringing colour, texture and flavour to meals, fruit and vegetables are high in fibre and many nutrients – too many to list here! Children need a variety of fruit and vegetables because each has a unique combination of vitamins, minerals and antioxidants. The easiest way to achieve variety is to include a mixture of colours every day. (See **Chapter 8: Training tastebuds**.)

Is juice a good replacement for fresh fruit?

Fresh fruit is better for your child than juice. Fruit juice contains some nutrients, but most of the fibre has been removed. By drinking fruit juice your child can consume a large amount of 'fruit sugar' without feeling full, which adds kilojoules and can be bad for their teeth. If your child drinks fruit juice, limit the quantity to ½ cup each day. Also limit dried fruit, because the sticky, concentrated sugar can cause tooth decay. (See **Chapter 10: Phasing out sweet drinks** for a helpful guide to reducing your child's juice intake.)

Lean meat, poultry, fish and legumes

Aim for 1–1½ serves of lean protein a day; serve fish twice a week and red meat 3–4 times a week.

1 serve =
- 65–100 g cooked meat (beef, veal, lamb, chicken or pork)*
- ½ cup (85 g) cooked lean mince*
- 80–120 g cooked fish*
- 2 eggs
- ½ cup cooked legumes (lentils, chickpeas, baked beans)

* To plan your shopping, multiply cooked weight by 1.25 to get approximate raw weight equivalent.

Why does my child need lean meat, poultry, fish and legumes?

These foods are high in protein, which is essential for your child to build muscle, bones and organs, maintain their immune system, produce hormones and repair DNA – and much more. Red meat is rich in iron, which is important for transporting oxygen around the body. Fish, seafood and red meat also contain omega-3 fats, which are important for nerve and brain function.

Omega-3

Omega-3 fatty acids protect against heart disease, stroke and joint inflammation (such as rheumatoid arthritis). Our bodies can't make enough 'long chain' types of omega-3s, so they need to come from the food we eat, such as fish, red meat and other food products that have added omega-3s.

Legumes

Legumes feature in the lean meat as well as the vegetable category because they are a plant food but also contain protein. Legume-based meals can be an economical and convenient option. Add variety to your meals by trying some of our bean recipes, such as spiced red lentil soup with cheesy subs (page 229).

Vegetarian diets

Vegetarian diets can be popular among teenagers, particularly girls. This happens for many reasons, such as a developing interest in food and health, for ethical, environmental or religious reasons, or sometimes as a way of asserting independence. This might concern some parents who are not familiar with a vegetarian way of eating, but with careful food choices a vegetarian eating pattern can support normal growth and development in children and adolescents.

If your child does decide to become a vegetarian, encourage them to eat healthy amounts of fat-reduced dairy foods or calcium-enriched soy foods, eggs (try omega-3-enriched, which are available at most supermarkets), legumes (such as beans and lentils), wholegrain breads and cereals, fruits and vegetables, nuts and seeds, and polyunsaturated or monounsaturated margarines and oils. If you are concerned about your child's nutrient needs or any weight loss, consult a health professional (such as a dietitian or doctor) to assess their diet.

Fat-reduced dairy foods

Aim for 2–3 serves of fat-reduced dairy foods per day.

1 serve =
- 1 cup fat-reduced milk, or calcium-enriched dairy alternative
- 200 g fat-reduced yoghurt
- 40 g fat-reduced cheese
- 1 cup fat-reduced custard

Why does my child need dairy foods?

Dairy foods are very nutrient-rich and an important source of calcium and protein. Childhood is when the body builds bones – they grow in size and strength (this is called bone density) – and the bone density your child develops now will impact the strength of their bones right through to old age.

Other foods also contain calcium, either naturally (such as bony fish and almonds) or added during manufacturing or processing (such as calcium-fortified soy drinks). While calcium-fortified dairy alternatives (such as soy drinks) can contain a similar level of calcium, they are not equivalent in terms of the other nutrients that dairy foods provide.

Fat-reduced dairy foods have similar amounts of calcium and other nutrients as full-fat products, but they are lower in kilojoules and saturated fat. 'Reduced-fat' milk (with 1–2 per cent fat content) and other fat-reduced dairy foods are suitable for children aged 2 years and older. Milk plays a smaller role in what your child consumes after the age of 2, so they don't need the extra kilojoules from full-fat dairy foods. By age 5 your child should be consuming either 'reduced-fat' or 'low-fat' milk (with less than 1 per cent fat content) and other fat-reduced dairy foods. The following table illustrates the difference in fat content in different types of milk.

Type of milk	Percentage of fat per 100 ml milk	Grams of fat per 100 ml milk
Full-fat milk	4 per cent fat	4 g
Reduced-fat milk	1–2 per cent fat	1–2 g
Low-fat/skim milk	less than 1 per cent fat	less than 1 g

Switching to fat-reduced dairy products is a simple way to limit the amount of saturated fat your child consumes.

What does it mean if my child is lactose intolerant?

Lactose is the naturally occurring sugar in cow's milk. The lactase enzyme in our small intestine normally digests this sugar. Some people do not make this enzyme, or have very low levels, so the lactose sugar is not properly digested and this causes bloating, stomach pains and diarrhoea.

People experience varying severity of lactose intolerance – some may only have symptoms after a large glass of milk, but not after a small glass. A simple way to manage lactose intolerance is to drink lactose-free milk, which is commonly available in supermarkets as fresh and long-life milks. Lactose-free milk has the same amount of calcium and protein as regular milk. People who are lactose intolerant can usually tolerate yoghurt and hard cheese because they have less lactose than regular milk.

Does my child have a cow's-milk allergy?

Some children develop an allergy to the proteins in cow's milk. It most commonly shows up as eczema (a skin irritation), diarrhoea and/or vomiting, face swelling, hives or wheezing and in severe cases may cause anaphylaxis. An allergy to cow's milk can only be managed by completely eliminating cow's-milk and dairy products from a child's diet. Children with a diagnosed cow's-milk allergy need alternative sources of calcium, such as calcium-fortified soy-, rice-, goat's-milk and other soy products such as custard or yoghurt, tinned salmon (with small edible bones), nuts (almonds, brazil nuts, hazelnuts) and wholegrain breads and cereals. Because cow's-milk allergy can occur with other food allergies, alternative calcium sources need to be chosen carefully. Most children grow out of this allergy by the time they reach age 4.

If you are concerned about your child's reaction to dairy foods, seek the advice of your doctor or a dietitian.

Oils, nuts and seeds

Aim for 6–8 serves a day.

1 serve =
- 1 teaspoon oil: vegetable, sunflower, safflower, corn, flaxseed, olive, canola or peanut
- 1 teaspoon margarine (low-salt, polyunsaturated or monounsaturated)
- 1 tablespoon nuts/seeds
- 1 tablespoon avocado
- 1 teaspoon nut paste
- 2 teaspoons mayonnaise

Why does my child need 'good' fats?

Some 'good' fats – such as polyunsaturated and monounsaturated oils and soft margarines – are essential to any healthy eating plan, because they provide nutrients such as vitamins E, A and K needed for vision, blood clotting and immune function. 'Good' fats also have a unique role in the outside layer of the cells in the body, especially brain cells. But remember, all fats are energy dense – they have about twice as many kilojoules per gram than carbohydrate and protein.

Why limit saturated fats?

Saturated fat raises cholesterol and forms fatty plaques in blood vessels of the heart, which can cause heart attacks and strokes. The gradual build-up of these fatty plaques begins in childhood, so limiting saturated fat is an important habit to form from a young age.

A healthy eating pattern will naturally include a small amount of saturated fat from foods such as dairy foods, meat, poultry and nuts. This is fine because a small quantity is not harmful and these foods provide many beneficial nutrients. The amount can be minimised by choosing fat-reduced dairy products and removing the visible fat from meat and skin from poultry.

Foods high in saturated fat to avoid include fried foods, butter, dairy blends/spreads, cream, creamy sauces, processed meats (such as sausages,

meat loaf and salami), coconut milk or cream, biscuits, cakes, pastries, chocolate and foods containing pastry (such as sausage rolls, pasties and pies).

The table below shows how healthier alternatives can lower your child's saturated-fat intake.

High saturated-fat food	Grams of saturated fat	Lower saturated-fat alternative	Grams of saturated fat
1 meat pie, pastie or sausage roll	15	1 meat and salad sandwich	4
1 serve of coconut-based curry	21	1 serve of Asian-style noodles with vegetables	5
1 doughnut	10	1 iced finger bun	2
1 Danish pastry	16	1 fruit scone	2
1 cup regular ice-cream	9	1 cup fat-reduced ice-cream	5
1 cream-filled biscuit	5	1 plain sweet biscuit	1
10 squares (40 g) chocolate	7	10 grapes	0

'Sometimes' foods

'Sometimes' foods are all the foods and drinks that don't fit into the basic food groups because they are low in beneficial nutrients and too high in energy, saturated fat, sugar and/or salt. They include foods that can be eaten at mealtimes and as snacks. 'Sometimes' foods might fill you up but they don't offer the nutrients you or your child needs.

Does my child need 'sometimes' foods?

Your child doesn't need 'sometimes' foods, but it is okay to offer them occasionally as part of a balanced eating pattern. If you do offer these foods, consider three key things: the type (is there a better option?), the frequency (should you set a daily or weekly limit?) and the serving size (could you share one serving between a few people?).

'Sometimes' foods*		
'Once a week' foods	**'Once a day' foods**	**Basic food group alternative**
1 small packet potato crisps or baked biscuit shapes (20 g)	10 rice crackers 20 g pretzels	3 wholegrain dry biscuits 1 cup popcorn made using corn kernels 1 corn on the cob
1 'fun size' chocolate bar (20–30 g) 6 squares chocolate or carob 10 jelly babies, chocolate- or yoghurt-coated foods	1 muesli bar 1 fruit bar (without yoghurt or chocolate coating)	1 piece fruit 1 small handful raw nuts, seeds and dried fruit mix
1 slice rich cake (such as butter cake, cheesecake, mudcake, cream-filled cake, chocolate cake)	1 slice plain, un-iced cake (such as banana cake, apple cake, tea cake, 'cake type' muffins)	1 slice fruit bread 1 English muffin 1 wholemeal crumpet 1 slice french toast
2 party-sized meat pies, pasties or sausage rolls 1 slice thin-crust pizza 1 hot dog in a bun 1 hamburger 1 small serve hot chips	1 commercial vegetable-filled filo roll 1 cheese-topped roll 1 grilled fish burger 1 savoury muffin	1 toasted sandwich 1 meat and salad roll baked beans on 1 slice toast 1 baked jacket potato topped with salad and grated cheese
3 golf-ball-sized scoops regular ice-cream or gelato 1 stick ice-cream	3 golf-ball-sized scoops fat-reduced ice-cream 1 icy pole	200 g fat-reduced yoghurt 200 g fat-reduced custard 3 golf-ball-sized scoops fat-reduced frozen yoghurt
1 small bottle (300 ml) soft drink or sports drink 1 glass (300 ml) cordial or fruit-flavoured drink	1 small bottle (300 ml) artificially sweetened 'fizzy' drink 1 glass (300 ml) artificially sweetened cordial	water 1 glass fat-reduced milk 1 small fruit smoothie ½ cup (125 ml) fruit juice (one a day)

*See **Risk of choking** box on page 116.

'Sometimes' foods are classified into two categories, based on how they are offered.

- 'Once a day' foods have a moderate kilojoule content but are low in nutrients, and many are high in salt. One small serve from this group can be included once a day.
- 'Once a week' foods are very high in kilojoules and very low in nutrients. If your child eats them, keep the amount to one small serve once a week.

Consider how the 'once a day' and 'once a week' approach might apply across a whole week and in different situations, and factor this into your meal and snack plan. For example, think of 'once a day' as also meaning 'seven a week', so when your child attends a party they might consume five 'once a day' foods in one afternoon. Make foods from the basic food groups the first choice so that there is scope to enjoy celebrations or special occasions. The table opposite shows some common examples of the different types of 'sometimes' foods – and some healthier alternatives from the basic food groups. See also the **Food rewards and bribes** box on page 47.

Food allergy and food intolerance

Many Australian children are affected by allergies, although not all are caused by food. Food allergy and food intolerance are different. Allergies involve the immune system and are relatively uncommon, but in extreme cases can be life threatening. Food intolerance is more common, and although it makes a child feel sick, it is generally not life threatening.

Common food allergies

Children can be allergic to one or more foods, and allergies are not always permanent. In fact most children grow out of them by age 5. It is important to know what foods contain the allergen your child reacts to so that those foods are avoided. The most common food children have an allergy to are:

- dairy foods
- eggs
- peanuts
- fish and shellfish
- soy beans, soy milk and soy flour
- wheat, which is in bread, cakes and biscuits
- some berry fruits such as strawberries.

Common food intolerances

Food intolerances are generally caused by chemicals that occur naturally in food, such as salicylates, amines, glutamates and sulphur-containing preservatives. Identifying which chemical is causing the reaction can be difficult because the problematic food chemical is often in a variety of foods, and because the reaction can vary depending on the amount of food chemical consumed.

Symptoms

The symptoms of an allergic reaction can include swelling, hives, eczema, diarrhoea and/or vomiting. In the most severe cases it can cause a life-threatening response called anaphylaxis, which can develop minutes after contact with even small quantities of the particular food. Symptoms of food intolerance can include hives, headaches, bowel upsets and wheezing or breathing difficulties.

If you think your child has a food allergy or intolerance, it is important that you seek the advice of your doctor.

Food additives and behaviour

Some food additives have a role in maintaining the safety of our food. They may also be used to help improve the flavour, texture and appearance of foods. Additives include preservatives, flavourings and colourings and Food Standards

Australia and New Zealand (FSANZ) controls the types and amounts of each additive permitted in food.

For most children additives are safe to consume, although a small number of children are intolerant to certain food additives. Some parents worry about the effect additives may have on their child's behaviour. While this is a current topic of research, at present there is not enough evidence to show clearly that additives have a negative effect on a child's behaviour. There is a small amount of research that suggests certain combinations of additives may adversely affect behaviour in some children.

Food additives must be listed on food labels, so parents can make the choice to avoid additives if they want to. Eating fewer 'sometimes' foods and more fresh fruit and vegetables is one way to avoid food additives.

Related information

See **Chapter 9: Keeping an eye on snacks** and **Chapter 10: Phasing out sweet drinks** for useful tips and step-by-step guides to help you provide healthier snacks and switch your family from sugary drinks to water.

leading an active lifestyle

Being active is just as important as healthy eating for your child, regardless of their age, size or shape.

Think back to your childhood. Chances are you walked or rode a bike to school and ran around with kids from the neighbourhood each afternoon until the sun went down. You were probably on the move most of the day. Now, however, children spend much less time being active, and this is affecting their health and wellbeing. Parents today have many more obstacles to face when it comes to ensuring their children lead active lives: work responsibilities, extracurricular activities, concerns for their children's safety, and the dominance of computer games and television to entice kids indoors.

Your child needs regular physical activity to strengthen their muscles, heart, lungs and bones; develop their motor skills, flexibility, posture, balance and coordination; achieve and maintain a healthy body weight and reduce their risk of cardiovascular disease and type 2 diabetes as adults. An active lifestyle will also help your child develop social skills and confidence. If your child enjoys being active, they are more likely to carry these habits and health benefits into adulthood.

Your role as a parent

One of the best things you can do for your child is to model an active lifestyle and provide them with lots of opportunities to move and play every day. If they see you being active they'll grow up understanding that this is a fun and normal part of life. It's also a great way to have family time, or some one-on-one time for you and your child.

You can play a major role in building your child's confidence and developing their skills – if your child feels good about their abilities they are more likely to participate in physical activity. Children don't need to be 'good at it' to enjoy participating, but they do need to feel supported and encouraged. When they are still learning, take the time

to help them practise skills, such as throwing and catching a ball. As they grow they may prefer to learn from others, and you can contribute by talking about their progress, providing moral support and encouragement, enrolling them in lessons or transporting them to activities. It's never too early or too late to start; your child will benefit from your support at any age.

How active should my child be?

The following guidelines indicate the minimum amount of time your child should spend being active. Remember that there are many ways to 'be active' and they don't have to involve lots of sweating and exhaustion afterwards! Think of being active as anything that involves moving – the less you and your child sit still, the better.

Preschoolers (3–5 years)

Preschoolers should be active for several hours every day. This will mainly involve supervised unstructured play, such as building a cubby house in the backyard, playing on equipment in a park, or indoor activities such as dancing. They might even 'help' you with household chores like sweeping and gardening. Under your supervision they can also engage in active transport, which might include walking to the shops or riding a bike to the park. Avoid keeping your child in a restrained seat such as a car seat or pram for more than an hour at a time.

Children and adolescents (5–18 years)

Children need to undertake at least 60 minutes (and up to several hours) of moderate to vigorous activity every day. Ideally this should be made up of a mixture of moderate activity (such as brisk walking, skateboarding, surfing, dancing or hide-and-seek) and vigorous activity (such as running, football, netball, soccer or swimming). Children aged 12–18 should aim for 20 minutes or more of vigorous activity and 40 minutes or more of moderate activity three to four times a week. The 60 minutes (or more) don't have to be reached all in one go – they can be spread over the day, and the more the better.

Example of building up 2 hours of moderate-to-vigorous physical activity in a day

Ride to school	10 minutes
Play handball at recess	10 minutes
Short game of basketball at lunchtime	15 minutes
Athletics practice after school	45 minutes
Ride home from school	10 minutes
'Shooting hoops' in the backyard	30 minutes
Total	**2 hours**

Once your child has undertaken an hour's moderate-to-vigorous activity, it doesn't mean they can sit on the couch for the rest of the day! Encourage active versions of things they enjoy doing – for example, suggest backyard cricket rather than playing a cricket computer game. Set aside some time each day that is spent outdoors.

Less screen time, more play

The amount of recreational time children spend at the computer or watching television and other screen-based entertainment should be limited to 2 hours a day. For children aged 2–5 this should be no more than 1 hour a day, and children under 2 years should spend no time on screen-based activities. Television, DVDs, console games, computers, the Internet and hand-held electronic games (including mobile phones) all stop children being active. While most of these activities have some educational or social benefit, the trick is to strike a balance. Watching a movie together may be a time to bond with your child, but ensure that this falls within the daily 2-hour limit.

More than half of primary school students and more than 70 per cent of secondary school students spend over 2 hours a day on recreational screen activities. Talk to your child about why it is important to limit their screen time each day, and focus on cutting down entertainment screen time. Teach your child to prioritise their viewing.

Television and snacking

Snacking while watching television provides a double whammy for unhealthy weight gain: firstly they are sitting still and not burning energy; secondly, they can consume a lot of kilojoules through snack foods and sugary drinks.

Related information

See **Chapter 14: Reducing screen time** and **Chapter 15: Becoming an active family** for useful tips and step-by-step guides to help you take positive steps towards a more active family today.

ages and stages of childhood

Childhood is a journey of gaining experience and independence. Your child needs your support in different ways at each stage.

As your child grows, they change from being completely dependent on you to being able to care for themselves. Knowing more about each stage will help you understand your child's needs and how to encourage them to form healthy eating and activity habits. This chapter provides some specific things to do and look out for at key stages of your child's development.

Toddler and preschool years (2–5 years)

Learning to be active

Toddlers and preschoolers have lots of energy for play. Playing is a time for them to learn different movement and coordination skills. Encourage your child to take the lead and explore, and aim for them to be playing actively for several hours a day. To boost the amount of time they are moving, avoid keeping your child in a restrained seat such as a car seat or pram for more than an hour at a time. For short trips, let them walk instead of using the stroller. Screen time should be limited to 1 hour a day. (See pages 30–1 for suggestions of the type of play suitable for your preschooler.)

> ### Helping children be active
>
> As parents you have an important role in helping children to be active by providing safe space and equipment to be active. Helping children to set up and start off an activity, and checking in regularly, can also get children being active and keep the activity going for longer.

Nutrition tips

Food is a common way preschoolers express their emerging independence. They are still learning about food, flavour and texture, which means they may want to explore, touch, taste, smell and watch others eat food before trying it themselves. To help them with this process, introduce a variety of foods, establish a meal and snack routine, be guided by their appetite, and eat the same meal as your child so they can learn by observing you.

Make mealtimes a team effort by sharing the decisions with your child: you decide what healthy meals and snacks are offered and when, and your child decides which parts of the meal they eat and when they've had enough. (See **Parent provides, child decides** on page 48.)

Your child's appetite will vary from day to day. When they are offered only nutritious food, they know how much they need to eat, so don't force them to eat when they are not hungry. (See **Balancing appetite and activity** on page 10.)

Establish a meal and snack routine by providing three meals and two or three snacks served at about the same time each day. (See **Follow a meal and snack routine** on page 43.)

Primary school years (5–11 years)
Being active

Your child will be able to perform many movements now, including bike riding, swimming, running and jumping. Their ball skills such as throwing and catching will also be improving. They will continue to have lots of energy. Coordination, flexibility, balance and endurance can vary between children and will improve with practice. Your child needs at least 60 minutes (and up to several hours) of moderate to vigorous physical activity every day.

Your child will now be embracing their independence but they still need you to ensure their play time is safe. Introduce and reinforce safety rules for outdoor play, such as road rules, safe boundaries and using safety equipment such as helmets when riding a bike. If you can, provide equipment that encourages them to be active, and inspire them to adapt household items for play too. Remember that free play is important, so try not to over-schedule their time. Your involvement can also be useful, especially to get activities started.

At this stage some children are ready for organised sport, but others may want to wait a little longer. Children who are not confident in their physical abilities and coordination may shy away from organised sport. If this sounds like your child, explore options that play to their strengths and interests. If they want to improve their skills, be there to help them learn. If your child does participate in sport, encourage them by watching their games and praising them regardless of the outcome. Recreational screen time should be limited to 2 hours a day.

Nutrition tips

This is an age when the influence of friends, peer pressure and media can grow stronger. While school and friends play a role in your child's life, you remain the main influence on what your child chooses to eat: you decide what healthy meals and snacks are offered and when. If your child requests 'sometimes foods', remind them of the rules you have set regarding these foods. In Australian children the average intake of soft drinks more than doubles around this age, so it is important to reinforce that water is the best drink.

Continue the routine of providing three healthy meals and two or three nutritious snacks served at the about same time each day. Encourage your child to become more adventurous with foods and to frequently try new things. Share mealtimes with your child as often as you can, and help them learn about food and cooking by involving them in food shopping, planning and preparation.

Secondary school years (11–18 years)
Staying active

The amount of physical activity children undertake dramatically decreases in secondary school. This is especially noticeable in adolescent girls. Why? For some adolescents, sport isn't seen as cool. It can also become too competitive for teens who are not confident in their sporting ability. Even if your child enjoys sport and physical activity, they may feel pressure to dedicate most

of their spare time to study. That doesn't leave much time for being active, but they still need at least 60 minutes of moderate to vigorous physical activity every day.

Help your child find a balance between schoolwork and recreation. For example, taking active breaks during homework can help their study, because physical activity can help them relax and concentrate, as well as boost their self-esteem. Encourage them to spend 15 minutes every hour stretching or skipping rope. They can also use active transport, such as cycling and walking, rather than relying on you to drive them everywhere – this has the added benefit of encouraging them to show responsibility and independence.

Your child may enjoy trying something new with their friends, such as athletics, kickboxing, dancing, yoga, sailing, tae kwon do or gymnastics. Alternatively, you can do something active with your teen, such as going for an early-morning bike ride or jog.

Weekends and school holidays are common times when screen time skyrockets – especially for teenage boys. Recreational screen time should be limited to 2 hours a day. (See **Chapter 14: Reducing screen time** for tips on cutting your teen's screen time.)

Nutrition tips

The intense growth that occurs during adolescence will increase your child's appetite. It is especially important during these times that they fill up on nutritious foods rather than 'sometimes' foods at meal and snack times. (See **Chapter 9: Keeping an eye on snacks**.)

Encourage all teenagers to eat red meat 3–4 times a week to meet their iron needs. Eating fat-reduced dairy foods 3 times a day is also important for strong bones. Continue to encourage water as their main drink.

It is around this time that adolescents start spending more time away from home, which can interfere with meal and snack routines. When they are at home, continue to eat together as a family at the table. To encourage them to eat at home rather than buying takeaway, you may need to be flexible with mealtimes. If they are going to be late, set aside a portion of the family meal for when they get home. When this isn't possible, help them make healthy choices outside the home.

Continue to involve your child in food preparation, which will teach them responsibility and important planning and food-preparation skills.

Sleep for teenagers

Generally, teenagers need between 8 and 10 hours' sleep a night. Unfortunately most teenagers do not get enough sleep, resulting in daytime tiredness, which can affect concentration, school performance, mood and general behaviour.

The changes associated with puberty mean that some teenagers experience a shift in their body clock. This makes it difficult for them to fall asleep at a reasonable hour at night (their body clock is telling them it is still time to be awake) and then difficult to wake up in the morning (their body clock is telling them it is still time to sleep). Many teens try to 'catch up' on sleep over the weekend, but this can actually make it harder for them to get enough sleep at the right times on weekdays.

Share the following tips with your teenager to help them into a regular sleep pattern where they will get sufficient rest.

- Stick to a consistent sleep routine. Try to keep school-day and non-school-day wake times (and bedtimes) within 2 hours of each other.
- Avoid caffeine in the afternoon and evening.
- Expose yourself to as much bright light (natural and artificial) as possible in the mornings.
- Undertake a relaxing activity immediately before bed. Switch off television and computer screens 30–60 minutes before bed.
- Limit daytime naps to around 20 minutes.
- Keep bedtime free from electronic distractions such as TVs, computers and mobile phones.

Related information

See **Part 2** for step-by-step guides to help you encourage healthy eating and activity habits in your whole family.

a parenting tool kit

Raising healthy, happy children takes a marathon effort. Having support and some practical parenting strategies can make it easier.

As parents, you are the leaders (and teachers) of your home. Just as you teach your child how to ride a bike, how to say 'please' and 'thank you' and how to get to school on time, you also teach them eating and activity habits that have a lasting influence.

While parenting is extremely rewarding, it can also be the hardest job you will ever do. You must be a counsellor, boss, bank, taxi driver, chef and all-round magician, yet you receive little or no training for such an important and complicated role. Along with all the joy and laughter, it's understandable if you sometimes question whether you are doing it right or if you could do better. Parenting does not always come easily – all parents learn on the job.

Here are five things to remember about being a parent.

- There is no such thing as the perfect parent.
- You are not alone; all parents struggle at times.
- You don't need to have all the answers.
- Successes and mistakes are all part of being a parent.
- Don't be too hard on yourself; celebrate when things go well.

The good news is that there are things you can do to be a more positive, confident, effective and consistent parent – a proactive parent. This chapter provides you with tools and strategies to make your role a little easier, from managing tantrums and enforcing a curfew to setting a limit on TV viewing and encouraging children to eat vegetables!

Laying the groundwork

Before we discuss specific skills that may help you to embrace a healthy family lifestyle, we need to introduce three key areas that form the foundation of proactive parenting: looking after yourself, working as a team and fostering good relationships.

1. Looking after yourself

While it is natural for you to want to make your child the top priority in your life, one of the most important things you can do as a parent is to take care of yourself. We all need balance in our lives, so although you may initially feel a little guilty about taking time out for yourself, it can help you be a better parent.

It is important to dedicate time and attention to the other key relationships in your life: remember that as well as being a parent you are a spouse/partner, daughter/son, sister/brother, friend or workmate. Also take the time to do things that make YOU feel good. This could be something simple like reading a magazine, going for a walk or chatting with a friend. Eating well and being active can lift your mood and improve your energy levels to help you balance all the competing parts of your life. And finally: ask for help when you need it – and accept help when it is offered.

2. Working as a team

Families come in a variety of shapes and sizes. No matter what the situation, if there are two (or more) people involved in raising a child, life will be easier if they work as a team.

Communication is vital when you are trying to create a happy, healthy home environment. Discuss with your partner (or others involved in raising your child) the things that are important to you both as parents, in a general sense and when dealing with specific situations. Discuss issues you don't agree on and make a decision about how to approach these issues if or when they arise in your family, and then back each other up.

It's easy to get caught up in the constant job of parenting, but it is just as important for you and your partner to support each another's interests and wellbeing. When you see that your partner is stressed or tired, offer extra support and reassure them that you are in this together. Encourage your partner to take some time for themselves, and also make time for just the two of you (you might have to schedule it in!) as partners as well as co-parents.

> **Helpful hint**
>
> If you can't remember the last time you had some child-free time with your partner or friends it's time to do something about it! Get together with friends who also have children. Set up a system in which you look after their children for an evening so that they can go out, and then they look after your children while you have a night out. Set up a roster: you could try for once a month – one month you get to go out; the next month your friends get to go out.

3. Fostering good relationships

All children need to feel secure and loved by their parents in order to learn and develop to their full potential. There are some simple things you can do to build a healthy relationship with your child. Be available whenever you can. If your child wants to talk to you or show you something, interrupt what you are doing and give them your undivided attention. This doesn't need to mean long periods of time – brief but regular lets your child know you are there. When your child talks to you, look at them, restate what you hear by putting your child's feelings into words and ask specific questions – this will show your child you are interested in what they have to say. You can never give your child too much warmth and affection. Share positive physical contact (hugs, cuddles, tickles, kisses) with your child every day and tell them how much they mean to you.

A positive relationship with your child can make teaching healthy eating and activity habits – and making changes to your family's lifestyle – a lot easier. Some habits (such as eating together as a family or being active together) not only teach your child about food and activity, but can also provide valuable opportunities to communicate.

Proactive parenting – key skills

Once you have laid the groundwork, there are some specific parenting skills that can help you be a more positive, effective and consistent parent – we have outlined five key skills below. You are probably already practising many of these skills, but seeing them written down together is often a useful reminder.

To help you to make healthy changes to your family's eating and activity habits, these parenting skills are applied in **Part 2: Making changes**. Look for the symbols throughout the book as reminders of these key skills.

Modelling

One of the most valuable things you can do for your child is be a good role model. After all, you are one of the most important and influential people in your child's life.

Some of the ways you teach and influence your child are easy to see: you know when you have taught your preschooler to write their name. You have probably observed your child behaving in a certain way and thought, 'Wow, that's just like me!'

At the simplest level, role modelling involves demonstrating desirable behaviour through your own actions. If you want to encourage your child to say 'please' and 'thank you', then you need to say these too. If you lead a healthy, active lifestyle, your child will be more likely to adopt this lifestyle too.

Role modelling is about more than actions. Your child also learns attitudes and beliefs from you. Think about your attitudes towards healthy living, and how these are absorbed by your child. Do you enjoy trying new foods? Do you prefer family meals at the table with the television off? Do you see physical activity as more of a chore or a pleasure? Your child will pick up on your attitudes and use them to form their own beliefs.

Monitoring

Children need to grow up in a safe environment. In the early years monitoring is all about keeping a close eye on your child to ensure their immediate surroundings are safe, they are getting all the nutrients they need to grow, and so on. As your child becomes more independent, monitoring is also about being aware: you need to know where your child is, whom they are with and what they are doing. Monitoring adolescents isn't always easy, particularly when they are becoming more independent, but it can also let your child know that you care about them and are interested in their life.

The aim of monitoring is to allow you to recognise when your child may be in danger or need extra support. It can prompt you to take action early to help your child and prevent problems developing.

In order to encourage healthy lifestyle behaviours that are suitable for your family, you need to be aware of your child's current behaviour patterns. The **Making changes** chapters in **Part 2** of this book ask you to begin by monitoring your family's behaviour patterns – for example, knowing how much television your child watches each week, what times of the day they watch it and what else is happening in the home at those times. Knowing what your family is doing helps you decide what (if anything) needs to change about your family's habits and lifestyle.

Setting boundaries

All families need some boundaries or rules. Boundaries help your child learn what you expect of them and provide a guide to behaving appropriately. The boundaries you set will be influenced by your values and beliefs and also by the age of your child.

The key to setting effective boundaries is to keep them simple. Before you set a boundary ask yourself: How important is this? Am I willing to follow through with consequences if my child breaks this rule? Stick to the issues that are important to you.

Boundaries should apply to all children in the family, although they might vary depending on age. Where appropriate, they should also apply to parents so you can model the appropriate behaviour. For example, if the rule is 'No television until dinner and homework are finished', it is unfair if you watch television while you cook dinner.

Your child is more likely to stick to rules that are specific, easy to understand and stated in a positive way. Rather than 'Don't leave the bathroom in a mess', ask your child to 'Hang up your towel and put your dirty clothes in the washing basket'.

You may want to include your child in a discussion on rule setting. Writing down and displaying rules for the family to see can prevent arguments down the track.

As with most aspects of parenting, consistency is paramount. Boundaries that are not consistently enforced by both parents are confusing for children. Your child is more likely to stick to the boundaries if they know you mean what you say, and will follow through with consequences if rules are broken.

Encouraging desirable behaviour

When you focus on your child's positive behaviours you will encourage them to behave this way again. When you see your child behaving in a way you like, give praise, and be sure to describe exactly what it is you like – 'Liam, I was very pleased with the way you spent the afternoon playing outside' – rather than focusing on your child –'Liam, you are fantastic!' This helps your child learn what it is you are pleased about and means they are more likely to repeat the desirable behaviour.

Try to avoid concentrating on your child's 'bad' behaviours. Aim to give more praise than criticism every day, and provide plenty of opportunities for good behaviour. Identify the times that most often lead to challenging behaviour in your family and work out in advance what you can do to encourage your child to behave appropriately. For example, if having the television on in the mornings causes your child to dawdle and make everyone late, turn it off and make a family rule of 'No television in the morning'.

Children are more likely to do things they have seen other people doing, so by modelling the desirable behaviour you want to see, your child has the opportunity to mimic it.

Managing resistance

No matter how hard you and your child try, there are going to be times when they challenge your decisions around family eating and activity patterns. This will be particularly obvious when you attempt to make changes to the way things are currently done in your family. Resistance is your child's way of seeing if you are serious about the changes – 'Does Mum really mean no sweet drinks at dinner time, or no television until homework is finished? If I keep nagging, maybe she will give in.'

If you are consistently using the positive parenting strategies of modelling, monitoring, setting boundaries and encouraging desirable behaviour, hopefully you won't need to deal with resistance very often.

When your child does test the boundaries, it is important to stand your ground. Once you have decided on your family rules, stick to them! Your child might not like the new rule of only 30 minutes a day on the game console, but if you are consistent in enforcing the rule, the nagging will eventually subside.

When you decide on consequences for rule-breaking, make them clear to your child, then apply them consistently – by both parents, on all occasions. The consequences need to be fair, and they should relate to the behaviour. For example, if your child reaches their agreed daily television limit, a logical consequence would be asking them to turn it off. Ensure this happens and ask them to remember the rule the following day.

Remember that praising your child for sticking to the new family rules will encourage them to continue behaving in this way.

These symbols provide a reminder of the 5 key parenting skills we have just outlined. These are used in each of the **Making changes** chapters in **Part 2** along with a specific example of how they apply to each change.

 Modelling

 Monitoring

 Setting boundaries

 Encouraging desirable behaviour

 Managing resistance

making good food available at home

Making healthy foods the easy choice for your family and enjoying the social aspects of mealtimes reinforce positive messages about food and eating even when life is busy.

Homes are the 'classrooms' for your child to learn lifelong lessons about preparing and enjoying healthy foods. Forming these habits at home has a positive influence on what your child chooses to eat as they grow and become more independent.

To get healthy eating habits off to a good start, stock your kitchen with the right foods. This goes hand in hand with following a meal and snack routine, planning a weekly menu and shopping for the required foods.

Follow a meal and snack routine

Most parents appreciate the value of sticking to certain routines, and mealtime routines are one of the most common. If your family finds it hard to eat meals at regular times, consider the common interruptions to your schedule. Do you struggle to serve dinner on time during the week because of work and after-school commitments? To manage this, try to serve meals that can be prepared on the weekend and then reheated on a weeknight, or prepare something quick and easy. (See our **Slow-cooked meals to keep** and **Almost instant** recipes in **Part 3**.)

The benefit of eating breakfast, lunch and dinner at regular times also applies to eating between meals. Constant grazing can interfere with a child's appetite; a break between eating will help your child to recognise their true hunger signals. So if your child gets hungry between meals, offer one morning snack and one afternoon snack at about the same time each day. If your child is used to grazing between meals it may take them some time to adjust to eating just one between-meal snack, so make this change gradually. (See **Chapter 9: Keeping an eye on snacks**.)

Plan a weekly menu

Planning a weekly menu will make it easier to follow a regular meal routine. Many families have some pattern, such as a curry on Sunday night, fish on Tuesday night, and so on. It's fine to follow a fairly repetitive pattern, as long as the meals include a variety of foods from the basic food groups (see page 19) and are prepared using healthy cooking methods (see page 115). Introducing a new dish or varying a current favourite can make mealtimes interesting and expose your child to new ingredients, flavours and cuisines.

Work smarter not harder
Serve everyone in the family the same meal. Children don't need special kids' food. **Chapter 8: Training tastebuds** provides some practical advice for helping the whole family enjoy the same meal.

When planning your weekly menu, focus on one meal at a time. It's usually easiest to start with planning breakfast for the whole week, then do lunches, followed by snacks and then dinner. Refer to the food group guidelines (see page 19) when you plan each meal. Consider the following points when planning your weekly menu.

- Breakfast and lunch are usually similar each day.
- Morning and afternoon snacks are an excellent opportunity to offer fruit and vegetables, and fat-reduced dairy foods.
- For the evening meal, focus on vegetables, some lean protein and wholegrain bread or grains such as rice or pasta. Plan to serve red meat 3–4 times a week and fish twice a week.
- Dessert is optional. If offered, it should be fruit based, perhaps served with fat-reduced yoghurt or custard.

The following example uses colour coding to show how meals fit the food-group guidelines. For extra inspiration, we refer to some recipes in Part 3 of this book and include lots of variety. This doesn't mean you always have to follow recipes or include as much variety on a daily basis – only you know what best suits your family.

	Breakfast	Morning snack	Lunch	Afternoon snack	Dinner	Dessert/ supper
Food group guidelines	2 serves bread/cereal 1 serve fat-reduced dairy	1 serve fruit	2 serves bread/ cereal 1 serve fat-reduced dairy ½ serve protein 1 serve vegetable	1 serve bread/ cereal 1 serve vegetable	1 serve protein – 3 red-meat meals a week 2 fish meals a week 3 serves vegetable 1 serve bread/cereal	1 serve fat-reduced dairy 1 serve fruit
Monday *(Home from work late)*	Muesli with milk and yoghurt	Apple	Salmon and pea quiche (recipe page 179) Tub of fat-reduced yoghurt	Crackers and beetroot dip (recipe page 152)	Spaghetti bolognese (recipe page 232) with garden salad (recipe page 213)	Banana with fat-reduced yoghurt
Tuesday *(Sports practice tonight)*	Weet-Bix with milk	Pear	Wholemeal sandwich with ham, cheese and tomato	Tomato on toast	Vegetable omelette (recipe page 159) on toast	Fat-reduced custard with cinnamon apple (recipe page 138)
Wednesday	Muesli with milk and yoghurt	Grapes	Multigrain sandwich with chicken, avocado and corn Cheese cubes	Wholegrain crackers with carrot and chickpea dip (recipe page 152)	Baked fish with tomato, onion and lentils (recipe page 217)	Fat-reduced yoghurt with strawberries
Thursday *(Swimming after school)*	Weet-Bix with milk	Melon balls	Wholemeal roll with grated cheese, tuna, celery and mayo	Wholemeal English muffin with honey and banana	Taco filled with salad and left-over bolognese sauce (recipe page 232)	Baked vanilla custard (recipe page 261)
Friday *(Children help with dinner tonight)*	Muesli with milk and yoghurt	Container of 'Two fruits' mix	Egg and ham pie (recipe page 146)	Spiced red lentil soup and toast (recipe page 229)	Pita pizza (recipe page 249) with chickpea and tomato salad (recipe page 245)	Fat-reduced yoghurt with tinned peaches
Saturday	Multigrain toast with Vegemite Glass of milk	Banana	Mushroom, spinach and feta mini frittata (recipe page 184) with toast Glass of milk	Cheesy vegie muffin (recipe page 149)	Yummy fish burger (recipe page 218) with vegie slaw	Fat-reduced ice-cream with tinned apricots
Sunday	Wholemeal crumpets with grilled cheese	Grilled fruit swords (recipe page 256)	Salt-reduced baked beans on toast Banana and strawberry smoothie (recipe page 133)	Cheesy vegie muffin (recipe page 149)	Roast lamb and traditional roast vegetables (recipe page 212) (Make bolognese)	Fat-reduced yoghurt with pear

If you do not offer your child dessert/supper, provide a serve of fruit at breakfast and/or a serve of fat-reduced dairy with their afternoon snack.

Write a shopping list

Use your weekly menu plan to write a shopping list. A list will speed up shopping and help you save money by avoiding spontaneous purchases and buying too much food. Stocking the right quantity of healthy food at home will mean you are less tempted to resort to expensive, unhealthy takeaway meals and snacks.

Remember to list not only the items you need to buy but also the quantities. For example, how many pieces of fruit will you need if the whole family has fruit for morning snack every day? Be sure to stick to your list when you are doing the shopping!

Make healthy foods easy to access

When your child starts to choose some of their own food, make it easy for them to make healthy choices. Put a fruit bowl in a prominent place. Keep a container of chopped salad vegetables and a tub of vegetable dip in the fridge. Prepare mugs of soup that your child can reheat. Use container sizes that your child can manage, such as 1-litre milk cartons rather than 3-litre cartons, and make sure lids are easy to remove. Keep water bottles in the fridge if your child prefers chilled water. Put suitable snack foods in the pantry in a place they can easily see and access.

Spring-clean the pantry

Take stock of the food and drinks in your home. The amount of 'sometimes' foods (see page 24) kept at home will influence how often these foods are eaten. The good news is this principle also works in reverse: when the pantry and fridge are filled with foods such as fruit, vegetables, fat-reduced dairy and wholegrain foods, that's what your children will eat.

Clear your pantry, fridge and freezer of the 'sometimes' foods you want your family to eat less frequently. For example, if your family agrees that they will share one packet of potato crisps a week, only buy one packet – once the crisps have been eaten, there won't be any more in the pantry and therefore no more temptation to eat too much of this 'sometimes' food.

Mealtime atmosphere

Mealtimes are not just about healthy eating; they are an opportunity for your child to learn about socialising, and a time for you to set a good example by eating the same healthy meal as your child.

Make it a priority to sit at a table to eat meals together. (If your child eats earlier than you, join them at the table while they eat.) Avoid distractions such as the television, toys and mobile phones during mealtimes. Focus on encouraging conversation and teaching your child to socialise.

It's never too early or too late to start involving your child in meal preparation, setting the table and cleaning up. Everyone wins: you get some help and they learn valuable cooking and organisational skills.

Food rewards and bribes

Many parents are aware of the power of food when it comes to influencing children's behaviour. It can keep them occupied when they're bored, or calm them when they're upset. Many parents find that food can be a good bargaining tool – when the children ask for ice-cream you know they'll clean their room or eat their vegies to get it. Perhaps you question whether it is a good idea to use food as a bargaining tool but you do it because it works and it achieves peace for the family. The children are happy, you get what you want – is that so bad?

Rewards or incentives can be effective in the short term. Children (and adults) will learn a new behaviour quickly when it is linked to a reward they value. And in a world of abundance, food has become a common way to manage children's behaviour, especially in public. In the long term, however, using food in this way can lead to excess consumption of non-nutritious foods, as well as give your child ammunition for pester power.

Encouraging desirable behaviour does not have to involve food. Think about what else your child enjoys, such as going to the park, spending time with friends, talking on the phone, or non-food trinkets they value (for example, stickers and stationery, books and magazines). Don't underestimate the power of simply spending quality time with your child as an alternative reward to food. (See also **Chapter 8: Training tastebuds** and **Chapter 9: Keeping an eye on snacks**.)

Parent provides, child decides – a healthy family lifestyle is a team effort

The way we encourage children to eat good food and be active is just as important as the type of food and activity opportunities we provide. Be clear about the roles and responsibilities you and your child have regarding their eating and activity patterns.

It is *your* job to decide:

- the number and type of meals and snacks your child will be offered
- the times meals and snacks will be available
- the amount of food available for meals and snacks
- the transport, sport, play or screen opportunities available to your child
- the play and sporting equipment available.

It is *your child's* job to decide:

- if they are hungry at meal and snack times
- how much, if any, of the food offered they will eat
- what activities they will undertake in their spare time.

Be alert to some common ways we encourage children to eat well or be active that can actually undermine our best intentions in the long term.

'Good boy for eating everything'

This message encourages your child to eat even if they are full. Many of us were taught to finish everything on our plate and now find it hard to break that habit, even if that means eating too much. When your child is offered nutritious food, they are able to use their appetite to guide how much they need to eat, so don't push them to eat more.

'I'm hungry!'

We need food for energy and nourishment, but food can also offer distraction, comfort or escape, for adults and children. If children are allowed to eat for these reasons they do not learn to do other things to meet these needs. Having a meal and snack routine helps avoid 'non-hungry' eating – if your child asks for a snack outside of regular meal or snack times you could offer a drink of water or suggest an activity to address boredom. Remind them when the next scheduled meal or snack is. If they *are* really hungry they will accept a snack of your choice.

'It's good for you'

This message can be ineffective to encourage children to eat healthfully. Children relate more to the here and now – 'It tastes good!' – than to long-term messages about future health. Healthy food preferences can be encouraged by the here-and-now approach and by repeated exposure to small amounts of the food (see **Chapter 8: Training tastebuds**). Encouraging familiarity can also be helpful, so talk to your child about the taste, texture and colour of different foods you would like them to embrace.

'I end up making three meals – just to keep everybody happy'

Making meals to cater to the preferences of different family members can create battles, stress and extra work at mealtimes, and it is a lost opportunity for your child to learn about healthy eating by sharing the same meal as the family. Asking your child what they want also means getting an answer of 'chips' when you were hoping for 'broccoli'. Keep your child's likes and dislikes in mind, but remember that your role is to decide what foods are served. Offer specific or 'limited' choices, such as, 'Would you like an orange or an apple?'

'I'm bored – there's nothing to do!'

Part of growing up is learning how to occupy our time, entertain ourselves and undertake the activities of daily life; one way your child learns these skills is by watching you and other members of the family. Make play equipment visible, provide a list of after-school or weekend activity suggestions, or get the ball rolling by helping them to start an activity. This can also help reduce your reliance on the ultimate babysitter – the television.

> **Related information**
>
> See **Chapter 9: Keeping an eye on snacks**, **Chapter 11: Starting the day with breakfast**, **Chapter 12: Preparing healthy lunches** and **Chapter 13: Making evening meals easier** for useful tips and step-by-step guides to help you provide healthy meals and snacks.

making changes

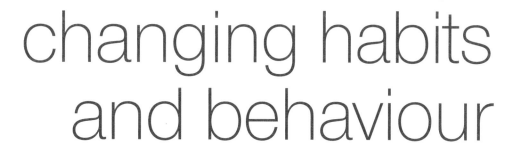

changing habits and behaviour

Understanding why you want to change a habit and knowing how to set realistic, achievable and measureable goals will provide you with a strong base to start making changes.

Are you ready to make a change?

Part 1 of this book assists you in identifying areas you may wish to change. The following chapters provide you with practical ideas for changing specific behaviours or habits to improve the health and wellbeing of your whole family. Read through the healthy habits we cover and think about what you would like to achieve for your family. Some of these things you are probably doing really well already; others you may wish to improve. Every home is unique, so choose goals that are most relevant to you and your family. Don't try to make all the changes at once – instead, pick a behaviour to start with and give it a go. Once you are happy with a change, consider the next behaviour you want to move on to.

A healthy lifestyle takes commitment, but you can do it!

Have you ever tried to alter an entrenched behaviour or habit? If so you will know how challenging it can be. Why is it so hard? Many of our habits become automatic, so changing them takes time, patience and perseverance, as well as a shift in attitude.

Changing habits usually involves learning new skills, which can be tricky. Think about when you learnt to ride a bike. The only way to get better is to practise the skill over and over. The good news is that the more you practise the easier it becomes – it's the same for your child: at first they may resist changes to their established habits, but if you persist they will get the hang of it.

Here we give you some key strategies to make changing easier. These strategies are used throughout the following eight chapters in Part 2, and they can also be applied to other habits you wish to change in your family.

Why are you making changes?

To successfully make changes to your family's health and wellbeing, you have to want to do it, and the first step is to work out why you are making these changes.

Make a list of the areas in your life that you think would benefit from change. What are the pros and cons of each change? In what ways will your family be better off if you make a change compared with your current behaviour? Are there any downsides or challenges to making a change? Keep this list somewhere handy so you can remind yourself often. There is an example of a pros and cons list in **Chapter 9: Keeping an eye on snacks**.

Imagine yourself having made the change. How will you be different? What impact will it have on your family? How will your child benefit? Think of people you know who have made similar changes. Consider these people your role models. Do they have any tips or strategies that could help you? For motivation, each of the following chapters in **Part 2** has a **Setting the scene** section with reasons for making a change.

Where should you start?

Before you can change a habit, you need to know where you are starting from. This can be more difficult than you might think, because often habits become so automatic that we don't recognise how often they occur. Identifying your starting point helps you track your progress and see when you make improvements.

One of the best and easiest ways to work out your starting point is to monitor a habit by keeping a written record. There are three key things to look out for while you monitor.

- How often does the behaviour occur? (Your child consumes an average of three sugary drinks a day.)
- When does the behaviour occur? (After school and at dinner time.)
- What else is happening while the behaviour occurs? (Your child is watching television.)

Monitoring will be most successful if you are honest and thorough. Don't cheat! Record every instance of the behaviour as soon as it occurs. Keep your record somewhere that is easy to access. You could try using a small card that you keep on you at all times. Or keep a chart on the fridge. Sometimes simply keeping track of a behaviour can result in a change.

Think of monitoring as gathering evidence. Monitoring will help you become more aware of the factors that are keeping the habit strong and then plan the most effective strategy for change. For example, planning to cut down on sugary drinks by simply limiting them at dinner time won't be very effective if these drinks are mostly consumed after school when your child is allowed to help themselves. In this case, a better strategy would be to focus on changing what happens after school.

Each of the chapters ahead provides advice about monitoring under the heading **Where do I start?**

What should you aim for?

Having the right goal for you and your family is important. While you can draw inspiration from friends who have made similar changes, remember that your family is unique and you need to adapt methods and strategies to suit your lifestyle. Following are some important things to keep in mind when setting your goals.

Don't let anyone else tell you what to do

Change has to be something *you* want, which is why you need to choose your own goals. In the chapters to come we suggest a main goal that describes the ideal situation – but this may be a long way from your starting point. So, in addition we provide some short-term strategies that are more specific stepping stones towards the main goal. These are ideas to get you started. If these are not realistic or suitable for you, discuss the issue in your family and come up with a goal that better suits your situation.

Make your goals realistic and achievable

The trick is to set a goal that is slightly more than what you are doing now, but not so far that there is no hope of achieving it. Having an achievable goal means that it is not only something that you want to achieve but something that you are able to achieve. Once you have achieved it, set another goal that progresses a little further towards the main goal and challenges you a little more.

Be specific

Goals should be stated clearly so that you know exactly what you are trying to achieve. 'Eat healthier' is not specific enough; 'Serve a salad or vegetables with every evening meal' is a specific

goal. You also need to be able to tell when you have achieved your goal. For example, 'Eat better' or 'Get fit' are not useful because you can't tell when you have achieved them. Instead, 'Be able to run 5 kilometres in 30 minutes' is a goal for which you can identify a final outcome, and know when you have achieved it.

Break them up

Achieving the main goal will be easier if you break it up into a series of short-term goals. Smaller goals or specific strategies will help you make progressive improvements that will move your family closer to reaching your main goal, and will also give you a chance to reward yourself for small successes.

Example

Main goal: The whole family will stop drinking sugary drinks.
Short-term goal: Replace fruit boxes with water in my child's lunchbox.
Short-term goal: Replace cordial with artificially sweetened cordial at family dinner time.
Short-term goal: Replace artificially sweetened cordial with water at family dinner time.

Make your first goal achievable – enjoying some early success will motivate you to keep working towards your next short-term goal and the main goal.

Write goals down and share them

Writing your goals down can increase your chances of success. Display your list somewhere you will see it often. Tell your family and friends about your goals and enlist their help to achieve them.

Making the change

As with most challenges in life, you have a greater chance of success if you plan and prepare. Before you get started, ask yourself the following questions.

- Are you realistic about the work involved in achieving your goals? Accept that it won't always be easy for you or your family, and that it's okay to feel frustrated sometimes.
- What props do you need to achieve your goals? You might need extra information, or the right 'equipment' such as healthy snack alternatives or a list of activities to encourage physical activity.
- What support do you have and what support will you need? Is your partner on board and keen to help your family achieve your goals? What about other people who regularly spend time with your child, such as neighbours, extended family or babysitters?
- What challenges might you face? Which times will it be hardest to stick to the plan? Come up with some strategies and solutions in advance.

In the next eight chapters we provide strategies to help you get started under the heading **Making the change**.

Making changes at home and beyond

Children (and parents) will find it easier if any changes you are making in your home are consistent with the other places your child spends time (for example, at their grandparents' house or after-school care). If you can, engage all the people who are involved in caring for your child and explain to them what you are trying to achieve. For example, you could ask after-school carers to serve milk or water instead of cordial or fruit juice, or suggest that grandparents take the kids to the park for a treat instead of buying them an ice cream.

However, we know that this may not be possible for some families or in some situations. If it is not an option, remember that focusing on the things you can influence in your own home still makes a huge difference to your child's health and wellbeing.

Going the distance

Maintaining change in the long run can be difficult, so begin by accepting that setbacks along the way are normal and common. The important thing is not to give up. If you stumble occasionally, take some time to re-evaluate your goals and strategies to see whether and how they need to be adjusted. Think of a slip-up as a learning opportunity that means you are better prepared next time. Remember to pat yourself on the back regularly for your successes along the way. Throughout the next eight chapters the sections **Making it easier** and **Tricky situations** provide tips to overcome common barriers.

training tastebuds

It's natural that your child won't like some foods, but you can encourage them to broaden their food horizons and enjoy a healthy, nutritious, balanced range of foods.

Setting the scene

Have you tried hiding cauliflower in mashed potato or blending pasta sauce to hide the carrot? You are not alone. Few parents have a child who happily eats everything they are offered. While babies generally accept their parents' choices, toddlers and preschoolers show their emerging independence at mealtimes and bring their personalities to the table. For many children, fussiness and resistance to trying new foods are part of this stage of life or can be an issue at any age. Although it can be frustrating at times it is important to persevere, because the foods your child likes at a young age may influence what they eat as adults. Helping your child to enjoy a variety of foods is important for now and for later.

Just as children take time to learn to talk and ride a bike, they also take time to accept new tastes and textures. They can be suspicious of foods they have not tried before or that smell or look different from what they are used to, and they often take their cues from your behaviour. Think about it: do you enjoy trying new foods?

'Training tastebuds' is a process that can help your child move from not wanting to try something, to tasting it, accepting it and finally to liking it. While this is a useful strategy for introducing new foods, of course it won't work for all foods – your child will have preferences and dislikes. In this chapter we provide strategies to help you teach your child to enjoy trying new flavours and widen the variety of foods they enjoy. We have chosen vegetables as the example because it is a common issue for parents, but you can apply the technique to other foods.

Vegetable taste challenge

Researchers in the United Kingdom investigated if children's liking for a vegetable could change. When parents offered a vegetable **daily for two weeks**, liking improved in 62 per cent of children. As a comparison, when parents were simply given information about the importance of eating vegetables, only 31 per cent of children improved.

Where do I start?

You need to establish what types of vegetables your child eats; you can then select a new vegetable you want your child to try. Using the table below, tick all the vegetables your child likes and eats regularly.

Orange and yellow	White	Green	Purple and red
☐ Pumpkin	☐ Cauliflower	☐ Broccoli	☐ Eggplant
☐ Carrot	☐ Mushroom	☐ Spinach	☐ Red cabbage
☐ Corn	☐ Swede	☐ Zucchini	☐ Beetroot
☐ Sweet potato	☐ Potato	☐ Peas	☐ Tomato
☐ Squash	☐ Onion	☐ Beans	☐ Red capsicum
	☐ Leek	☐ Cucumber	☐ Radish
	☐ Parsnip	☐ Celery	
	☐ Turnip	☐ Green cabbage	
	☐ Fennel	☐ Green capsicum	
		☐ Asparagus	
		☐ Asian greens	
		☐ Brussels sprouts	

Think about the number of serves of vegetables your child regularly eats. Do they eat vegetables at lunch and dinner each day, as well as snacks? As an example, count the number of serves (1 serve = ½ cup vegetables or legumes, 1 cup salad or 1 medium (150 g) potato; for children under 5 years of age 1 serve = 1 tablespoon × age in years) they ate yesterday, and write them down on this table.

	Vegetable type	Colour group	Number of serves
Breakfast			
Morning snack			
Lunch			
Afternoon snack			
Dinner			
Total			

From the first table, are there any colour groups without any ticks? If your child is missing out on an entire colour group or groups, aim to introduce a new vegetable from that group. If all groups have at least one tick, you are doing well! The aim now is to expand the variety of vegetables your child eats in each group.

If all colour groups have a few ticks, variety of vegetables may not be a problem for your child. If this is the case, look at the second table to see whether they are achieving the recommended 5 serves of vegetables each day or 4 serves for

children under 5 years. You may want to increase how much they are eating by serving the vegetables at snack times, lunch and dinner.

What should I aim for?

Main goal: The whole family will be offered a variety of vegetables each day.

Remember
You can use the strategies in this chapter for other foods too. Is your child eating a range of foods from the basic food groups (see page 19)? You can modify your goals to target any of the basic food groups.

Short-term strategies:
- Increase your child's vegetable intake by serving vegetables at snack time, lunch and dinner.
- Offer your child a new vegetable from the colour table using the step-by-step plan over the page.
- Involve your child when you prepare the vegetable.
- Provide opportunities for your child to learn about the vegetable – they can plant seedlings, shop for it or choose a recipe using it.
- Show your child that you enjoy eating the vegetable.

Making the change
Just because a child does not like a food the first time it is offered does not mean they will never like it. Your child might need to taste the new vegetable 10 or more times before they accept

or like it. Remember that you should encourage your child to try new food, but never force them. The goal is to offer the new vegetable regularly.

Use the information you have gathered to choose a vegetable to introduce to your child. Avoid something you know your child really dislikes – it's best to begin with a vegetable you are confident they will grow to enjoy. Select a vegetable that is inseason – it will be more readily available, cheaper and have better flavour. Finally, choose one that can be easily prepared every day for the 2-week taste challenge. School-aged children might like to choose the vegetable for themselves.

Once you have chosen the vegetable, use the following step-by-step plan.

1. Introduce the idea of tasting new foods to your child. You could make this a tasting game. If your child is in upper primary school or older they might like to approach it as an experiment: 'Can we train our tastebuds to like a new flavour in 2 weeks?'
2. Familiarise them with the vegetable. Tell them what it is. Let them choose it at the shop – they might like to touch and play with it. Involve them in the preparation or cooking and then let them serve themselves. If your child is very fussy it might be better to prepare the vegetable in the same way each day, because two different preparation styles can seem as different as two different vegetables.
3. Offer a small amount of the vegetable every day for two weeks. Work towards encouraging your child to taste the new vegetable. You might need to accept that a tiny piece is all they will try at first. In some cases simply getting used to having the vegetable on their plate will be progress. For this exercise, you can offer the vegetable either at meals or outside of mealtime, and it doesn't need to be offered at the same time each day – choose the least stressful option.
4. Taste it together and show that you enjoy it. Your child is unlikely to try a new food if nobody else in the family is eating it; they need to see you (and any siblings) eating the food to know it's safe and enjoyable.
5. Don't make a fuss. Encourage your child to have a taste, but don't force them to eat it. If the experience is horrible the first time, it will make it harder the next day.
6. Focus on the vegetable rather than on their eating it. Comment on an interesting feature of the vegetable, like its colour or shape, how it feels to touch, or if it makes a crunching sound when you bite it.

Making it easier

Training the tastebuds is one approach. Consider these general tips to help your child embrace a wide range of foods, including vegetables every day.

Add other flavours and try different textures

Everybody's tastebuds are different, so prepare vegetables in a way that will excite your child's tastebuds. The preparation doesn't have to be fancy or time-consuming, but it might take a few tries to get the right option for your child. They might learn to like broccoli when it is soft and mushy, or crunchy in a stir-fry, or steamed, tossed in some herbs or spices or dipped in a little cheese sauce.

Don't offer bribes

Bribes can undo all your good work and get your child into the habit of only eating their vegetables if there's something in it for them. The focus should be on learning to enjoy vegetables rather than on a reward at the end.

Remember that it's okay for them to dislike some foods

There are going to be some vegetables (and foods) that your child may never really enjoy. If they eat a variety of different-coloured vegetables, it doesn't matter if they don't like *all* the orange or *all* the green vegetables. Remember, though, that tastes can change over time, so give your child the chance to re-try 'disliked' vegetables from time to time.

Make the most of the early years

Your child may initially be good at eating different foods and flavours but then gradually (or sometimes suddenly) become more discriminating. It's a good idea to take advantage of the time your child is more agreeable to eating a variety of foods by introducing many different textures and flavours. Children will learn to like certain flavours, especially the sour and bitter flavours found in some vegetables, the more they taste them. Think of your own experience learning to appreciate the flavours found in coffee, dark chocolate, wine, beer or an unusual spice.

Teenagers can learn to like new foods too

Repeated exposure is beneficial throughout childhood and even into adult years, so it's not too late to reintroduce foods that your teenager refused in the past. Cooking, shopping or going to the market together might be an enjoyable way to introduce something new. If you have served a non-preferred food, it is reasonable to expect your teenager to try at least a small amount.

Raising the profile of healthy foods

Many unhealthy foods have an advantage in the image stakes through clever advertising. What is your first choice of food for celebrations – vegetables or sweet treats? Children pick up on these messages, so it is important to show them that healthy foods aren't just the things they *must* eat. Link healthy food to special or positive experiences, so your child won't always automatically think junk food equals fun. For example, consider offering big chunks of juicy watermelon on a hot day, rather than ice-creams.

Tricky situations
Handling refusals of vegetables or new foods

If your child is hesitant to try new foods you will need extra patience and persistence. Try not to get frustrated. Avoid pleading with your child or entering into a debate about their eating. You may need to choose a different vegetable – something similar to a vegetable they like, such as pumpkin and sweet potato. Make sure your child sees you eating the vegetable. Don't pressure them to eat it the first time – they may first need to simply see it on their plate. When they do eat it, give them some praise. Don't punish your child for refusing a vegetable. If your child causes a scene at mealtimes, introduce a family rule about behaviour at the table, such as no pushing food away or complaining about what has been served; instead family members must say, 'No, thank you' when they don't want to eat something.

What if you have tried a similar approach before and it didn't work?

'Training tastebuds' can be a tiring and frustrating process, especially if your child continually refuses to try new foods. Some children need to spend time becoming familiar with a food before they will be brave enough to taste it. Remember your starting point. Progress can be the acceptance of a new food on the plate, willingness to have a tiny taste or even showing interest in the food. Generally two weeks should be enough time for your child at least to taste a new food, but of course not all children fall into this category. Some may need longer, so if you feel like you are getting nowhere, remember:

- minimise wastage by serving a small amount every day
- minimise effort by keeping preparation simple
- minimise frustration by not creating a fuss
- maximise success by being consistent and a positive role model.

Parenting tips for training tastebuds

 Modelling When you want your child to try a new vegetable, make sure you eat it with them. Show your child that you are willing to try new things too.

 Monitoring Know how many different vegetables your child is eating. Check whether they are eating a variety of coloured vegetables and foods from all the basic food groups.

 Setting boundaries Talk to your family about starting a rule that all family members will put at least a small amount of a new food on their plate. Let your child know that they don't have to keep eating something they don't like, but they will be encouraged at least to taste it.

 Encouraging desirable behaviour Remember to give your child lots of praise when they try new foods or show an interest in food activities such as cooking, growing herbs and vegies or going to the market or grocer.

 Managing resistance Prepare and share the same foods as a family. If you have agreed on mealtime rules, remind your child what is expected of them. Stick to these rules. Resist the temptation to make something different to cater especially for individual preferences or to offer bribes to entice your child to eat.

> **Related information**
> See **Chapter 4: Ages and stages of childhood**, **Chapter 6: Making good food available at home** and **Chapter 13: Making evening meals easier**.

keeping an eye on snacks

Snacks don't have to be 'junk' food for your child to enjoy them – there are plenty of nutritious, convenient and tasty options that can compete against the latest snack fads.

Setting the scene

A small snack between meals can be part of a balanced eating pattern and keep tummy rumbles at bay, but too often this turns into grazing, often on 'sometimes' foods that add unnecessary saturated fat, salt and sugar and can spoil your child's appetite for (and interest in) healthy meals.

It can be tricky to balance *what* your child eats between meals, *how much* they eat and *how often*. Snack foods are available anywhere, anytime and in growing serving sizes. There is also advertising to contend with and the persistent 'Can I have . . .' as children try to keep up with their friends.

Now is the time to give your child's snacks a makeover! In this chapter we provide strategies to help you encourage your child to eat nutritious, tasty food and drinks between meals – foods they find satisfying and fun, and you find convenient and not too costly.

of what your child eats between meals, keeping the following things in mind.

How often?

How many set or regular between-meal snacks does your child have each day? How often do they eat, drink (other than water) or graze outside meal or snack times? Do they help themselves to food or ask permission? Does your child eat snacks while they watch television or play on the computer?

What's on offer?

What food and drinks are available for between-meal snacks? How often does your child eat snacks that have been bought away from home, including at school? If your child is regularly cared for by someone else, what snacks do they eat then?

How much?

What is the serving size of food or drink for between-meal snacks? Do you use multi-pack portions or other strategies to serve small portions?

What about food as a treat or reward?

Do you offer your child food as a reward for good behaviour or as a treat to show affection? If so, what sorts of foods do you offer? What types of food are eaten at celebrations in your family? Does your child view these treat foods as special?

LEARNING RESOURCE CENTRE
The Oxford Academy
Sandy Lane West
Littlemore
Oxford OX4 6JZ

Snack fact

In our survey of Australian parents, 46 per cent of parents who were concerned about what their children ate or drank said that 'junk food' was the biggest worry. Between-meal snacks are a common time children eat these foods.

Where do I start?

You need to get a clear idea of the types of foods your child eats between meals, and why, so you can identify if and how changes need to be made. Review the past or coming week as an example

Food treats

Food is part of socialising and celebrating, and is also a common way we treat ourselves and our children. There are two things we need to keep in mind when we hand out food as a treat: how often do we use food as a treat, and what types of foods do we consider treats?

Treats used to be reserved for special occasions, but these days there seem to be many more reasons to treat ourselves with food: celebrations, visitors, family time, good days, bad days, it tastes good, we deserve it, it's just there. The downside to this approach is that treats have become so common that children don't always view them as special; in fact they often expect them. Here are some tips to keep these foods special.

- Teach your child that a treat is occasional, not every day, and should be valued and appreciated.
- Your child takes their lead from you, so think about the role food plays in your life as reward or comfort.

'Sometimes' foods (see page 24) have become synonymous with treats, but a treat doesn't have to be unhealthy, nor does it have to be food. Find healthier food and activity options that can be special for your family, such as the following.

- A banana smoothie or a Vegemite sandwich can be just as pleasurable as lollies or chips.
- Serving food in a different way can be the novelty for children. They love serving themselves from a large pot in the middle of the table, or compiling their own taco, hamburger or pizza.
- Make the most of local parks that have barbecues, or take a picnic to a special place.
- You can treat your child by spending special time with them: making a kite with Dad or playing a game or sport with Mum are alternative ways to treat your family and yourself.

Changing your child's snack habits can be a big challenge, particularly if your child is old enough to object to changes to their regular way of eating. We have set out over the page a list of the benefits of and barriers to changing what your child eats and drinks between meals. You will see that even though there are barriers, there are always tactics to overcome them. Use the table as a starting point to identify things relevant

Benefits of change	Barriers to change
One step closer to a healthy, balanced way of eating It will be easier for your child to accept healthy foods when they are not competing with highly flavoured fatty, sugary or salty options. **What else are you cutting out?** Your child will be consuming fewer food additives, colours and flavours by eating fewer processed snack foods. **They feel better on the inside and out** Teenagers tell us they feel a difference on the inside and out when they eat less junk food. **Make it a habit when they're young** You will find it easier to form and change habits when your child is young, so the earlier you start, the better.	**'It's beyond my control.'** No, it's not! As parents you have a very important impact on what your child chooses to eat, despite the influence of school, friends and advertising — especially when you change what is on offer at home. **'I don't know what to offer. Apples just end up in the bin.'** Remember that there are many inexpensive, easy and tasty snack ideas to tempt young tastebuds. See the ideas that follow, and try the recipes in **Part 3** of this book that can be used as between-meal snacks. **'I don't want battles.'** Try to think of it as short-term pain for long-term gain. The **Making it easier** section opposite highlights ways you can reduce your child's resistance to change. **'I don't want to deprive my child.'** Treats can come in other forms too! You can help your child see healthy snacks as treats.

to your family. You can also add your own pros and cons to change.

What should I aim for?

Main goal: The whole family will be offered up to three healthy between-meal snacks a day.

Short-term strategies:
Use the results from your review of your child's snacks to decide what you are aiming for and what you want to change. Here are some examples of snack-related strategies to get you started.

- Replace 'sometimes' foods with fruit, vegetables, wholegrain foods and fat-reduced dairy foods as between-meal snacks.
- Cut back on after-school grazing at home by providing one (substantial) nutritious snack.

- Reduce the number of nights each week dessert is offered, or only offer healthy options such as fruit and fat-reduced custard rather than ice-cream.
- Teach your child that 'sometimes' foods are something to enjoy occasionally.
- Reward good behaviour with an extra bedtime story, stickers or a game of Sunday backyard cricket, instead of food.

Making the change

The taste, convenience and appeal of common snack foods means the amount of snacks children consume can easily creep up, taking over from main meals. Consider the following five steps you can take to regain control of what your child snacks on between meals.

1. Set up a between-meal snack routine. Eating once between each main meal is enough for most children: something at recess or morning tea, and something for afternoon tea. Dessert/supper is optional.

2. Avoid 'sometimes' foods at snack time; instead, offer between-meal snacks from the basic food groups – wholegrain breads and cereals, fruit and vegetables or fat-reduced dairy foods. The box shows some examples to choose from.

3. Between-meal snacks should be smaller than a meal, but serve enough to satisfy your child until their next meal. (See page 19 for a guide to portion sizes for children.)

4. Get everybody on board, and make the changes with minimal fuss. Focus on the positives: 'Let's try one snack after school so you have more time to play,' or 'Let's try some new tasty snack foods'. Involve school-aged children by asking for their suggestions or by making a list together (but remember that you make the final decision).

5. Monitor additional snacks, such as ice-creams after swimming lessons or sweet buns when you go to a bakery. When your child has an additional snack they might not need the planned between-meal snack as well.

Morning tea/ recess: Fruit	After-school snack: Vegetables and wholegrains	Dessert/supper: Fat-reduced dairy foods or fruit*
Apple or kiwi fruit	Pumpkin, carrot and parsnip soup (recipe page 226) with wholemeal toast	Fat-reduced chocolate custard with sliced banana
Canned or stewed fruit snack pack	Tomatoes on wholegrain toast (recipe page 135)	Fat-reduced frozen yoghurt with warm stewed fruit
Banana	Wholemeal Salada with cream cheese and grated carrot	Fruit smoothie (recipe page 133)
Bunch of grapes	Multigrain English fruit muffin with honey	Fat-reduced vanilla yoghurt with canned apricot
Watermelon slices or balls	Carrot and chickpea dip (recipe page 152) with rye crackers	Grilled fruit swords (recipe page 256)
Fruit smoothie (recipe page 133) or fruit muffin	Corn Thins topped with tomato and grilled cheese	Fruit crumble (recipe page 258)
Box of dried fruit-and-nut mix	Wholemeal cheese and tomato scones	Baked vanilla custard (recipe page 261)

*If you do not offer your child dessert/supper, provide a serve of fruit at breakfast and/or a serve of fat-reduced dairy with their afternoon snack.

Making it easier

Consider the following tips to help your child embrace healthy snack options.

Limit 'sometimes' foods

'Sometimes' foods may be included in a healthy, balanced eating pattern (see **'Sometimes' foods** on page 24). Offer your child 'sometimes' foods sparingly to give them more flexibility to enjoy those foods at celebrations or on special occasions.

You can take simple steps to limit the serving size of 'sometimes' foods – after all, the larger the portion offered, the more your child is likely to eat. For example, serve cakes in thin slices rather than chunks, break chocolate into small pieces, share portions of baked goods and king-size snack options and purchase the smallest-size multi-pack snacks. Don't forget the value of simply not keeping these foods in your home!

Keep snacking and screen time separate

Watching television or playing on the computer when eating can distract your child from noticing their body's signals telling them they are full; this makes it easy to overeat. To reduce screen-time snacking, teach your child that snacks are to be eaten at a table (or at least away from the television and computer). Also keep in mind that while 'television and a snack' is a common family activity, it sends a mixed message to your child.

Healthy snacks can be fun

It can be easy to make healthy snacks fun. For preschool children, present their healthy snacks in fun ways, such as bite-sized pieces, colour groups or shapes. School-aged children are more likely to accept between-meal snack changes if they understand the change. Involve your child in counting the number of 'sometimes' foods they (or the family) are offered on a weekday, weekend day or at a celebration – and then discuss what healthier foods could have been offered instead. Make a list of these foods to try as between-meal snacks over the next school term.

Good habits don't need to stop at the front door

There are many occasions when your child needs their morning or afternoon snack away from home, but these don't have to interrupt your healthy eating plan. You can take something suitable from home, or if you need to buy snacks while you are out, choose the healthiest option – and teach your child to do the same. At the bakery they can choose a small fruit bun, cheese roll, pizza bread, fruit scone or grainy roll; at the greengrocer they can choose fruit or vegetables; at a cafe they can choose a fat-reduced smoothie or toasted cheese sandwich; and at a deli they can choose a tub of yoghurt, a sandwich, a piece of fruit or a salad.

Tricky situations
Battle of the will!

Have you ever had to do the grocery shopping while being pestered by your child to buy them the latest snack craze? It's understandable that we sometimes succumb to their nagging, but when we do, we show them that the rules about snacks are flexible. To control the snacks both inside and outside the home you need to be strong and consistent. For every request to buy an unhealthy snack, say to your child: 'It's not on the list, so it's not going in the trolley.' It may make for a few tough shopping trips, but your child should eventually learn to stop asking.

Getting others on board

Now that you are in control of the snacks at home, see if people outside the home who care for your child – grandparents, friends, childcare workers – can also follow this routine. It is easy and natural for grandparents to want to spoil their grandchildren, but keep them aware of your child's healthy-snack plan; you might even share some recipes (such as our smoothie recipes on page 133, muffins on pages 149 and 263 or banana pikelets on page 145) with them.

Weekends and school holidays

Weekends and school holidays are times when routine typically goes out the window. Try to maintain your regular meal and snack routine during these times to show that you are serious about these healthy habits. It may also make the transition back to school a little easier.

Parenting tips for keeping an eye on snacks

 Modelling Watch what you eat, role-model good between-meal options (including the night-time television snack!) and ensure that enough healthy snacks are on the shopping list and available in the kitchen.

 Monitoring Be aware of the types of food and drinks your child eats and drinks between meals. Count up how often your child has 'sometimes' foods each week, and plan ahead for celebrations or special occasions, so they can be part of their meal and snack plan.

 Setting boundaries Set a meal routine to encourage your child to have breaks in eating over the day. Talk to friends and family about these boundaries to get their support when your child visits. Have a family rule that encourages children to ask before they help themselves to food at buffets or when at a friend's house.

 Reinforce the positive Encourage enjoyment of everyday healthy snacks and treats such as sweet juicy peaches in summer, stewed rhubarb in winter, banana smoothies and cheese jaffles.

 Managing resistance Be consistent when dealing with pester power. While requests for junk food at the supermarket may initially increase, remember that every 'no' from you is one step closer to peace and quiet. With persistence, your child will learn that no means no.

Related information

See **Chapter 10: Phasing out sweet drinks** and **Chapter 12: Preparing healthy lunches** for useful tips and step-by-step guides to help you control between-meal snacks and 'sometimes' foods.
Chapter 17: Food and shopping guide and the 'bring a plate' recipe suggestions on page 252 may also be helpful.

phasing out sweet drinks

Your child can quickly develop a taste for sweet drinks, but phasing them out will help protect teeth and cut down on unnecessary sugar and kilojoules.

Setting the scene

The only drinks your child needs are water and milk, yet in Australia 2–3-year-olds consume on average 150 ml of sweet drinks (mainly juice) each day. This quantity increases as children grow – teenagers drink on average over 500 ml of sweet drinks (mainly juice and soft drinks) each a day.

The main problem with drinks other than water or milk is the kilojoules coming from sugar. Your child can easily consume a lot of sugar (and kilojoules) via sweet drinks because drinks don't fill them up the same way food does, and this can impact their body weight.

The other problem with sweet drinks is the damage they can do to your child's teeth: sugar encourages plaque to form on teeth, and the acid in carbonated drinks (even the sugar-free varieties) erodes tooth enamel. Water and fat-reduced milk are better options because of the fluoride in tap water (in many Australian cities and towns) and the calcium in milk.

In this chapter we provide strategies and tools to help you phase out sweet drinks and encourage your child to enjoy drinking water and milk.

Where do I start?

To help you decide on the best way to phase out sweet drinks, you need to know what types of drinks your child consumes, where they are consumed and why. Spend a few days observing and recording what your family drinks, keeping the following questions in mind.

What drinks are consumed?

Take note of the type and quantity of drinks your family consumes. Include soft drinks (regular and artificially sweetened), cordial, fruit juice, fruit-based drinks, sports drinks, energy drinks, tea and coffee. What size are the cups or drink containers?

When are these drinks consumed?

What time of day or occasion is associated with consuming sweet drinks? Are they mainly consumed at mealtimes or between meals? Are they consumed more on certain days, such as weekends or school holidays?

Where are these drinks consumed?

Does your child usually have sweet drinks at home, or in relatives' homes, at school, during sports practice or activities such as shopping or going to a movie?

Why are these drinks consumed?

Who serves these drinks? Who buys these drinks? Is your child allowed free access to these drinks or do they have to ask permission? Are some drinks automatically offered at certain occasions, such as juice at breakfast time, soft drinks at dinnertime, sports drinks after Saturday-morning sports games?

What should I aim for?

Main goal: The whole family will drink water to quench thirst. The only other regular drink offered will be milk.

Short-term strategies:
Use the results from your review of your child's drinks to decide what you are aiming for and what you want to change. Here are some examples of drink-related short-term strategies to get you started.

• Gradually reduce the number of nights each week you offer sweet drinks with dinner, until water is offered every night.

- Switch from fruit boxes to water bottles for your child to take to school three days a week, and continue to reduce the fruit boxes until water is offered every day.
- If your child is used to drinking cordial at home, switch to sugar-free cordial, and then gradually make the mixture weaker. Eventually progress to water.
- Reduce the amount of juice consumed to ½ cup a day by using smaller glasses and diluting juice with water.

Making the change

Completely cutting out all drinks other than water and milk may work for your family. You could go straight to step 4 for a no-fuss approach. If you would like to make gradual changes, follow this step-by-step approach, with each step moving closer towards the main goal. You might choose to start with one or more of the changes in steps 1, 2 or 3 and transition to step 4. It's up to you to decide how long you spend at each step and how gradually you introduce these changes.

1. Cut down on the amount of kilojoules from sweet drinks by:
   - switching from regular soft drinks to artificially sweetened soft drinks
   - switching from regular cordial to artificially sweetened cordial
   - switching from sugar-sweetened flavoured milk to articifially sweetened varieties or fruit smoothies
   - reducing the size of the glass used to serve sweet drinks

- reducing the number of glasses of juice consumed to once a day.

2. Reduce the sweetness of drinks by:
   - replacing artificially sweetened soft drinks with weak artificially sweetened cordial
   - diluting artificially sweetened cordial by adding more water and less syrup
   - replacing some artificially sweetened cordial with water or milk
   - diluting fruit juice with water so that no more than ½ cup is consumed a day.

3. Replace weak artificially sweetened cordial with water.

4. Replace regular and artificially sweetened soft drinks and cordial with water.

Making it easier

Consider these extra tips to help wean your child off sugary drinks.

Encourage your child to drink water

Make water easily accessible: keep water bottles ready for school lunches and around your home, and keep jugs of water in the fridge. Encourage your child to take a bottle of water from home when they go out. A special water bottle, fancy glass or straw might make drinking water fun. And if your child needs a little more convincing, they may like a slice of orange or lemon to flavour the water.

Remember fat-reduced milk as a drink

Your child needs 3 serves of fat-reduced dairy food every day, and fat-reduced milk is a great

alternative to soft drinks and cordial. They can create their own special drink by blending fat-reduced milk with a small amount of powdered flavouring or their favourite fruit. Smoothies make great snacks (see our recipes on page 133).

Tricky situations
Is juice a suitable alternative to fruit?

If your child refuses to eat fruit, offering juice isn't the ideal solution. Fruit juice provides some nutrients but very little fibre. It is important to address your child's reluctance to eat fruit – see

Chapter 8: Training tastebuds for practical tips. Limit fruit juice to ½ cup (125 ml) a day. This is an opportunity for you to be a good role model by eating fresh fruit.

Are sports drinks necessary?

Water is the ideal drink to quench your child's thirst. Children do not need sports drinks for hydration, even when the weather is very hot. Sports drinks contain added sugar, which can mean consuming unnecessary kilojoules without being satisfying.

You could limit your child's intake to one small sports drink per week, counted as their once-a-week 'sometimes' food. Alternatively, cut out sports drinks altogether – you could buy a special water bottle and/or add a dash of artificially sweetened cordial while they adjust to drinking just water.

There isn't a magic number for the amount of water your child needs to drink to stay hydrated, but as a general guide they should drink water frequently enough so they don't get to the point of feeling thirsty. They will need extra water during hot weather and when they are very active.

If children can get sweet drinks at friends' and relatives homes, is there any point changing what they drink at home?

Most of what your child consumes comes from home, so encouraging the right habits and taste preferences there is very important. Circumstances away from home are sometimes out of your control; you might have to accept these situations, knowing that what happens at home has changed for the better. You could provide your child with a suitable drink to take when they go to a friend's house, and speak to the other parents about ways they can support your plan. Discuss your expectations with your child when they are old enough to make responsible decisions and suggest ways to help them make better choices.

Parenting tips for phasing out sweet drinks

 Modelling Set a good example by making water your main drink.

 Monitoring Get to know the times your child drinks sweet drinks, to identify whether it is an issue at home, at school or during activities away from home.

 Setting boundaries Establish good drinking habits by offering only water or milk at meal and snack times. Set limits about other sweet drinks and talk about these boundaries with your family so they know what is expected of them.

 Encouraging desirable behaviour Encourage your child to enjoy water by serving it chilled, or in a special cup, and take water bottles with you when you leave home. Remember to praise your child when they choose water as a drink.

 Managing resistance In order to make the switch from sweet drinks to water easier, make gradual changes by decreasing the amount your child consumes (the volume and the frequency) and the sweetness of these drinks.

> **Related information**
>
> See **Chapter 2: The good food essentials** for a description of 'sometimes' foods and the importance of dairy products and fresh fruit.

starting the day with breakfast

Breakfast is an excellent way for your child to start the day. A healthy breakfast fuels their body for a full day of learning and activity.

Setting the scene

We all need a nutritious breakfast to perform at our best. Children's growing bodies and developing brains rely on a regular supply of sustenance; if they skip breakfast they go for a long time without the food that provides nutrients and energy – the time between dinner the night before and morning tea could be up to 16 hours! Unfortunately, missing breakfast is common for many Australian children, especially as they get older. For some children this is due to a lack of time, while for other (usually older) children it may be due to a lack of appetite.

Children who eat breakfast generally have a more nutritious diet. This may be because they are less likely to be hungry throughout the morning, which reduces the chances of snacking on high-kilojoule, low-nutrient foods. Eating breakfast can also help children concentrate for longer and perform better at school.

For many families mornings mean mayhem: parents rushing to get ready for work, trying to get children ready for school, packing lunchboxes, rushing to catch buses . . . does any of this sound familiar? In this chapter we provide strategies, skills and tools to help you reclaim control of your mornings and encourage your child to start the day with a healthy, tasty breakfast.

Where do I start?

You need to get a clear idea of how often your child eats breakfast, and what they eat. Answer the following questions by placing a tick in the appropriate box.

	YES	NO
Do I (and my partner) eat breakfast every morning?		
Does my child eat breakfast every morning?		
Do our breakfasts regularly contain wholegrain foods (such as wholegrain toast, muffins, wholemeal crumpets, or wholegrain cereals such as Weet-Bix, Weeties, Sultana Bran, oats or natural muesli)?		
Do our breakfasts regularly contain a serve of fat-reduced dairy (such as fat-reduced milk, fat-reduced yoghurt or fat-reduced cheese)?		
Do our breakfasts regularly contain fresh fruit?		
Do our breakfasts regularly contain fruit juice or other sugary drinks?		
Do our breakfasts regularly contain high-sugar/high-salt cereals?		
Do our breakfasts regularly contain fried foods (such as bacon, hash browns)?		
Do our breakfasts regularly contain full-fat dairy (such as full-fat milk, yoghurt or cheese)?		
Do our breakfasts regularly contain high-fat baked goods (such as croissants, pastries)?		

Ticks in the green boxes indicate great breakfast habits. Ticks in the orange boxes suggest room for improvement. If your ticks are mostly in the green boxes: well done, you are doing a great job! Use any orange answers as a guide to areas to change. If your ticks are mostly in the orange boxes, you might have a bit of work to do.

	Example: Jack				
Monday	1 Weet-Bix with sultanas and milk ✓				
Tuesday	'Not hungry' ✗				
Wednesday	As Monday ✓				
Thursday	As Monday ✓				
Friday	'No time' Sweet biscuit ✗				
Saturday	Coco Pops with milk and large juice ✗				
Sunday	French toast (multigrain bread) and Milo ✓				

Another way to monitor your family's breakfast habits is to fill in the chart above. Put each family member's name along the top and record each day whether they had breakfast and what they ate and drank.

If there are members of your family who do not eat breakfast regularly you could include a section on your chart to record the reason for not eating breakfast – 'not hungry', 'no time', etc. Gathering this evidence will help you when begin to make changes.

What should I aim for?

Main goal: The whole family will be offered a healthy breakfast every day that includes some wholegrain bread or cereal and fat-reduced dairy.

Short-term strategies:

Use the results from your review of your family's breakfast habits to decide what you are aiming for and what you want to change. Here are some examples of breakfast-related short-term strategies to get you started.

- For children over 2 years, replace full-fat dairy with fat-reduced options, including milk, yoghurt and cheese.
- Replace high-sugar cereals with low-sugar wholegrain alternatives such as wholemeal crumpets, toast and cereal. Add fresh, canned or small amounts of dried fruit for sweetness.
- Phase out fruit juice or limit to 125 ml (½ cup) a day.

- Incorporate vegetables such as mushrooms, tomatoes and spinach.
- Save 'treat' breakfasts – such as pancakes or bacon and eggs – for special occasions.

Making the change

A common reason for many families not eating breakfast is lack of time. Here are some steps to help you organise your mornings and ensure your child starts their day with a healthy breakfast.

1. Make sure you have appropriate breakfast foods at home – there is nothing worse than realising in the morning that you have run out of milk or bread, so check the night before! As a back-up, keep a loaf of bread in the freezer, and long-life milk in the pantry.

2. Do as much as you can the night before. Think about the things that slow you down in the mornings. How could you give yourself more time to prepare and enjoy breakfast in the morning? You could pack school bags, sign notes and homework diaries, check that everybody has their clothes/uniforms ready to go and even make school lunches and keep them in the fridge overnight.

3. Get a good night's sleep. It is much easier to get going in the morning – and have the energy to enjoy breakfast – if you have had enough quality sleep the night before. (See **Chapter 1: Watching your child grow** for more about sleep.)

How to choose a healthy breakfast cereal

Ready-to-eat breakfast cereals are very popular, especially among children. Cereals can be quick, easy and inexpensive, but are they always the best option?

As a general guide, cereals that resemble the original ingredient are a good choice – have you ever seen a chocolate-flavoured oat or wheat grain, or a bright pink, yellow or green rice grain? Healthy everyday cereal options are wholegrain and high in fibre but low in added sugar and salt. Examples include Weet-Bix, Weeties, untoasted muesli and porridge. You can also look out for cereals that have the Heart Foundation Tick as a guide to better choices.

You can increase the goodness of your child's cereal by not adding sugar; instead try fresh, dried or stewed fruit or fat-reduced yoghurt.

Making it easier

Consider the following tips to ease the morning mayhem.

The early bird . . .

If mornings are chaotic for you and your family, try getting everyone up 5–10 minutes earlier than usual. These extra few minutes can really make a difference.

Eliminate distractions

Set a family rule of no television in the mornings. Alternatively, you might allow your child to watch television only after all their morning tasks – getting dressed, eating breakfast, cleaning teeth, getting schoolbag organised – have been completed.

Get everyone to help out

Children can help prepare their own breakfast. Even preschoolers should be able to help in some way. Try assigning each family member a task. For example: one to get the cutlery and crockery, one to get the cereals, milk, bread and spreads, and one to clear the table after breakfast. Some of these jobs could be done the night before to save even more time.

When things don't go to plan

There are some days when things just don't go to plan. When this happens and you really don't have time to sit down to breakfast with your child, try having a breakfast on the run. Many fruits and toasted sandwiches are easily transportable; eating breakfast bars and breakfast drinks is not a great thing to do every day but it is okay to resort to them in emergencies.

Race the clock – a game to help children get ready in the morning

Making a game out of getting ready in the morning can really help. The idea is to reward your child for being ready on time. The reward could be a sticker or smiley-face chart, or a special activity with Mum or Dad such as a family bike ride or a trip to the park to kick the soccer ball.

1. Write a list of the tasks your child needs to do each morning. For younger children you might like to use pictures.
2. Display the list somewhere that you and your child can easily refer to it.
3. Agree on a time in the morning by which your child needs to be ready (you might like to use the oven or microwave timer to count down).
4. Encourage independence by leaving it up to your child to do what they need to do to get ready. Prompt your child to check the list if they are unsure what to do next.
5. Make sure you give lots of praise and encouragement when you see your child being independent.
6. If your child achieves all the tasks on the list before the time is up, they win!

Adapted from the Raising Children Network, raisingchildren.net.au

Tricky situations – adolescents and breakfast
'If I don't eat breakfast, I might lose weight.'

Many adolescents mistakenly think that skipping breakfast is a good way to lose weight or prevent weight gain. In fact, this can actually make it more difficult to maintain a healthy weight. If you suspect your adolescent is avoiding breakfast for weight or appearance reasons, talk to them about the role breakfast plays in maintaining good health and preventing unhealthy weight gain.

'I don't want any breakfast, I'm not hungry.'

Lack of appetite in the morning is a common reason given by adolescents for not eating breakfast. Try offering a nutritious drink instead – check out the smoothie recipes on page 133 in **Part 3**. Or talk to your teen about breakfast options they can take with them and eat on the way to school, such as a piece of fruit or a wholemeal crumpet, roll or sandwich.

'I just can't get him out of bed in the morning.'

Parents often report that their teenagers are extremely difficult to get out of bed in the morning. Many adolescents experience a shift in their body clock, making it difficult for them to stick to regular sleep patterns, and when they are dragged out of bed on a school day, they may not feel like eating breakfast. If this sounds like your teen, try to ensure they keep consistent waking hours, and limit weekend sleep-ins to within an hour or two of the time they have to get up during the week. (See also the **Sleep for teenagers** box on page 36 for more information.)

Parenting tips for starting the day with breakfast

 Modelling Show your child that you enjoy eating a nutritious breakfast as part of your daily routine.

 Monitoring Be aware of what your child eats for breakfast and how many days per week they eat breakfast.

 Setting boundaries Decide what are appropriate breakfast foods for every day and what foods or dishes are kept for special occasions. Only make healthy breakfast options available in your home.

 Reinforce the positive Praise your child for eating breakfast if this was not happening before. Encourage and praise their efforts for getting through the morning tasks and for helping.

 Managing resistance Try to find out more about why breakfast is not being eaten and offer solutions. For example, if it is lack of appetite you could try providing a healthy option that can be eaten a little later in the morning.

Related information

See **Chapter 17** for a food and shopping guide to help you select good breakfast items. There is a whole selection of breakfast recipes in **Part 3** for your family to try.

preparing healthy lunches

Children eat a third of their food during school hours, so what goes into their lunchbox is important. Children's lunches can be healthy, portable, easy to prepare – and enjoyable!

Setting the scene

Children need a variety of healthy foods to fuel their body and mind throughout the day. Start the day with a healthy breakfast and then follow up with a balanced, nutritious lunch.

A lunchbox should contain healthy foods and water, and provide the right amount to match your child's appetite. The photo on the next page shows the content of two different lunchboxes: both contain a sandwich, a drink, a piece of fruit and a few snacks, but the bread, sandwich filling, drink and snacks in the one on the right make it a much healthier option.

This chapter provides you with lots of ideas for healthy, enjoyable and filling school lunches. Many of these ideas can also be used on weekends and during school holidays, and for children who don't go to school yet.

A typical lunchbox contains:	
• Vegemite sandwich on white bread • 1 piece of fruit • Muesli bar, fruit roll-up or potato crisps • 2 sweet biscuits • Fruit drink or cordial	✓ Breads and cereals ✗ Vegetables/salad ✗ Lean meat or protein alternative ✗ Fat-reduced dairy ✓ Fruit ✗ Water **3 'sometimes' foods**
Healthy lunchbox contains:	
• Wholemeal sandwich with chicken, avocado, carrot and lettuce • Cubes of fat-reduced cheese • Cherry tomatoes • 1 piece of fruit • Bottle of water	✓ Breads and cereals ✓ Vegetables/salad ✓ Lean meat or protein alternative ✓ Fat-reduced dairy ✓ Fruit ✓ Water **0 'sometimes' foods**

Where do I start?

You need to get a clear idea of what types of foods your child eats for lunch at home and school, so you can identify if and how changes need to be made. Start by taking note of exactly what is going into your child's lunchbox and what happens on weekends. Use the chart opposite to record what your child eats for a week, including the contents of their lunchbox as well as any food and drink they buy from the school canteen or local shop during the day. Note whether any food comes home uneaten, sandwiches are made with white or wholegrain/wholemeal bread, your child eats vegetables or salad during the day, what they drink and how many 'sometimes' foods appear over the week. (See page 24 for more information about 'sometimes' foods.)

Typical Australian lunchbox

Healthy lunchbox

	Recess	Lunch	Drinks	Food bought – on the way to school – at recess – at lunchtime – after school
Monday				
Tuesday				
Wednesday				
Thursday				
Friday				
Saturday				
Sunday				

What should I aim for?

Main goal: My child's lunch will contain*:

- 2 serves of wholegrain bread and wholegrain cereals (for example 2 slices wholemeal/wholegrain bread or 1 cup rice or pasta)
- ½ serve of lean meat or alternative (for example 1 egg or 30 g tuna or leftover roast meat)
- 1 cup salad or ½ cup vegetables
- 1 serve of fat-reduced dairy (for example 1 cup milk or 40 g cheese or a 200 g tub of yoghurt or custard). Serve full-fat dairy for under 2s.
- Morning snacks will be based on fruit, vegetables and fat-reduced dairy.

* These portion sizes will vary depending on the age and sex of your child. If you need to increase or decrease the amount, keep the proportions the same. (See page 19 for more information about portion sizes.)

Short-term strategies:
Use the results from your review of your child's lunches to decide what you are aiming for and what you want to change. Here are some examples of lunch-related strategies to get you started.

- Replace fruit drinks with drink bottles filled with water.
- Reduce the frequency of white-bread sandwiches: begin by including high-fibre white or a combination of wholegrain

and white bread, then move towards only including wholemeal/wholegrain bread.

- Replace 'sometimes' foods such as crisps and sweet biscuits with tubs of fat-reduced yoghurt, cubes of fat-reduced cheese or fruit.
- Include some salad or vegetables in sandwiches or as a snack.

Sweet and salty snacks

Cakes, biscuits, slices, buns, bars, crisps, chocolates, lollies, pastries, soft drinks, cordials and juice are often high in saturated fat, sugar or salt. These don't fit in a healthy lunch.

Processed meat

Processed meats (such as ham, chicken loaf, smoked turkey and salami) may be a convenient sandwich filler, but they can also be high in salt and saturated fat, so avoid using them as an everyday lunch item. Instead try hummus, egg, leftover roast meat or cooked chicken.

Making the change

Your child's lunchbox doesn't have to contain different foods every day. If you find a healthy sandwich filling that is quick to prepare, inexpensive and enjoyed by your child, stick with it for a while. Add some fruit and a bottle of water, and that's just fine! Here are some quick, easy and healthy snack and lunch ideas. You can also try some of the recipes in **Part 3**. (See also Risk of Choking box on page 116.)

1. Offer healthy snacks based on fruit, vegetables and fat-reduced dairy, such as:

- grapes, cherries and strawberries
- cubes of watermelon, rockmelon, pineapple or kiwi fruit
- stone fruit such as apricots, peaches, nectarines and plums (cut in half and remove the stone)
- apples, pears and mandarins
- corn on the cob (try buying frozen corn pieces and microwave for a few minutes; children enjoy eating this cold)
- plain popcorn, either on its own or mixed with dried fruit
- cherry tomatoes
- canned or tinned fruit (in natural juices)
- a small carton of fat-reduced milk (plain or flavoured)
- cubes of fat-reduced cheese
- tubs of fat-reduced yoghurt and custard (avoid dairy desserts that have added sugary toppings and sprinkles).

2. Provide healthy and satisfying lunch foods, such as:

- sandwiches – see the recipes on pages 143–4 for filling ideas, such as chicken, avocado and corn, or roast beef, tomato and chutney
- savoury muffins (page 149), egg and ham pies (page 146) and corn and pea fritters (page 145) – make large batches and freeze lunch-sized portions to use during the week
- dinner leftovers such as homemade pizza (page 249), frittata (page 180) or quiche (page 179)
- our recipes for fried rice (page 197) or couscous (page 167) in small containers.

3. Encourage water as your child's main drink to keep them well hydrated throughout the day. Include a water bottle in your child's school-bag every day. In summer half-fill the bottle and leave it in the freezer overnight, then top it up with water in the morning: this will provide a lasting cool drink throughout the day and doubles as a lunchbox cooler.

Keeping it cool
To keep yoghurt and milk cool in summer, freeze it overnight or place next to an icepack or frozen water bottle in your child's lunchbox.

Making it easier
Consider the following tips to help your child embrace healthy lunch options.

Involve your child
Talk to your child about why you are providing different foods. They will find it easier to accept the changes if you include them in the shopping, allow them to choose what goes in their lunch-box (within healthy limits) and involve them in lunch preparations. Remember to praise your child when they have eaten something healthy for lunch – especially if it's a new food for them.

Plan ahead
Stock the freezer with dinner leftovers in small containers and other freezable snacks to grab on the go – this can save you time each morning and also provide back-ups if you run out of fresh ingredients. Take some time on the weekend to make lunchbox fillers: pop a large batch of popcorn or boil eggs to add to sandwiches; bake a large batch of savoury muffins (see recipe on page 149) and wrap them individually before storing in the freezer – these will defrost in a few hours, ready to be eaten for lunch.

Prepare the night before
There are some simple time-saving strategies you can employ to help ease the pressure in the mornings. The best option is to make the lunches the night before and store them in the fridge ready for the next day; this is particularly suited to lunches that include dinner leftovers. Depending on your child's age, they can help by getting fruit, filling water bottles, putting lunches in containers and putting ingredients away. They might even be able to make their entire lunch!

Play it safe
Take the following steps to ensure you prepare and store foods safely: wash your hands before preparing food and work on a clean surface and with clean utensils; store foods at risk of bacteria (such as meat, fish, milk and cooked rice and pasta) in an insulated bag next to an icepack or frozen drink; clean lunchboxes after every use and throw away perishable foods (such as dairy, meat, rice, pasta and dips) that are not eaten during the day. Consider using a lunchbox that is insulated or include an icepack inside a regular lunchbox, especially during warm weather.

Tricky situations
Dealing with peer pressure: 'I want to eat the same things as my friends.'
Having similar lunches to their friends might be important to your child, and they may resist the

changes you implement. It is important that you persist with the change to show that you are serious – their resistance will usually diminish over time. In the early stages you may need to talk to your child about why a nutritious lunch is important. It might also help to make healthier versions of the types of foods they are used to, such as switching from a piece of cake to a wholemeal fruit muffin. Start with one change, such as just changing the morning snack or just improving the drink.

Teenagers buying 'junk' for lunch

Keeping track of what your child eats can be difficult, particularly as they get older and start to choose their own foods. They often have their own money to spend at the school canteen or the local shop, which can make you feel like they are undoing all your positive changes. Concentrate on the things that do you have control of, especially the food available in your home.

To encourage your teen to pack a healthy lunch, stock your pantry and fridge with nutritious, tasty, easy foods – this might also include asking your teen what foods they want for lunch and involving them in the shopping. If they take food from home, ask them if it is enough – are they buying food because they are still hungry? And ask if they need more money to buy healthier foods – unfortunately salad rolls can cost more than hot chips or a pie, so you might need to consider whether you can increase your child's lunch money if it means they will choose the healthier

option. You could also suggest healthier choices, such as buying a finger bun rather than a doughnut, or a cheese-and-bacon roll rather than a pie or pastie.

What about lunch orders?

There have been great improvements to the foods available at many school canteens in recent years, but your child may still have access to 'sometimes' foods. If you complete a lunch order for your child, provide them with a smaller list of the healthier options to pick from. This allows them to enjoy the novelty of a school lunch order and encourages them to make healthy choices within boundaries you set. If your child places the order themselves, monitor what they order; ask what they have chosen and encourage healthy options. Avoid making canteen lunches a reward for your child taking lunches from home most of the time – this could encourage your child to like lunch orders more and home lunches less.

Parenting tips for preparing healthy lunches

 Modelling Lunchboxes are a great way to model healthy eating for your child. Remember to pack yourself a healthy lunch so that your children can see how it's done.

 Monitoring Keep an eye on what comes home uneaten, and talk about other healthy options your child could try. If your child has money to spend on food, ask them what they buy and talk about healthy choices.

 Setting boundaries Get your child on board by offering them some choice about what they take for lunch within the healthy limits you set.

 Encouraging desirable behaviour Work with your child, while keeping it simple for yourself. If your child is happy to stick with the same fruit for morning snack, that's fine.

 Managing resistance If you find certain foods consistently come home uneaten, ask your child why. They might not like that particular food, it could be too hard to eat, take too long to eat – or maybe they are simply not hungry enough to eat it all.

> **Related information**
>
> See **Chapter 6: Making good food available at home** and the **Food and shopping guide** in **Part 4**.

making evening meals easier

For busy families, the evening meal can be hectic and stressful. Whether you have minutes or hours to cook, it *is* possible to prepare a healthy evening meal to enjoy together.

Setting the scene

The afternoons and evenings are so busy: parents juggle work and family responsibilities – picking up the children from childcare or school, sport and music lessons, supervising homework and preparing for the following day. It's no wonder we struggle to find time to shop for and cook healthy evening meals. As children get older it may be harder to bring everyone together for dinner – and when you do, it can be hard to talk over the television. Despite this, most Australian families try to eat together most nights – 87 per cent of parents in our survey eat together at least five nights a week.

Evening meals are not just about food; they can be a great family time. Shared evening meals encourage better family relationships and open communication, more nutritious meals, healthier long-term eating habits and less tension within the home. Children who share meals with their family eat more healthfully and are at lower risk of obesity, exhibit fewer risk-taking behaviours and show better school performance. This may not be just because of the meal itself; it is also a time when your child can observe and mimic social skills, learn healthy eating habits and be exposed to a range of healthy foods.

Chapter 6: Making good food available at home outlined the steps needed to plan healthy meals. In this chapter we provide some extra tips to prepare nutritious evening meals. We also offer suggestions to help you and your family enjoy eating together.

Where do I start?

You need to focus on two areas: first, think about the meal – what food and drinks does your family have at dinner? Second, focus on the meal environment – how do you interact as a family during the meal? To identify if and how changes need to be made, use this table to record what and how your family eats in the evening for a week. Include as much detail as you can. This initial stage of monitoring will help you decide on the next step.

	The meal List each food item served at the evening meal. What proportion of the meal (or plate) did each item occupy? List any drinks, starters or dessert served.	**The food environment** Where was the meal eaten (at a table or in front of a TV, friends'/relatives', cafe)? Was anybody missing? Why? Note the mood (rushed, pleasant, tense). Anything else?
Monday		
Tuesday		
Wednesday		
Thursday		
Friday		
Saturday		
Sunday		

What should I aim for?

Main goal – the meal: The whole family will be offered balanced evening meals, including*:

- Vegetables – 1½ cups different vegetables for children 5 and older; for younger children use their age times 3 tablespoons for an approximate amount to offer at dinner time.
- Lean meat or alternative, the size of your child's palm (red meat 3–4 times a week, fish twice a week, alternatives such as white meat, egg or legumes on the other nights).
- Bread or cereal (about ½ cup cooked rice or pasta, noodles or couscous, or 1 slice of wholegrain bread or 1 medium potato).
- A small quantity (2 teaspoons per person) of healthy oils for cooking or in dressings.
- Water (or fat-reduced milk) to drink.
- Dessert is optional and will depend on what other snacks your child has eaten during the day. If you offer dessert, make it fruit, perhaps with fat-reduced custard or yoghurt.

* The serves listed here will vary depending on the age, sex and activity level of your child. If you need to increase or decrease the amount, keep the proportions the same. For example, aim to make vegetables half of the meal with ¼ meat (or alternative) and ¼ grain or cereal food. (See page 19 for food and quantity guides for your child and family.)

Short-term strategies – the meal:
Use the results from your review and the evening meal recommendations above to decide what you are aiming for and what you want to change. Select one or two meal components to work on at a time. Here are some examples of meal-related short-term strategies to get you started.

- Reduce the amount of unhealthy fats used in cooking (see **Chapter 16: Healthy cooking**).
- Increase the variety and quantity of vegetables served as part of the evening meal (see **Chapter 8: Training tastebuds**).
- When offering dessert, make it fruit-based with fat-reduced dairy products as an occasional accompaniment.
- Change the drinks you serve from sweet options to water (see **Chapter 10: Phasing out sweet drinks**).
- Reduce the frequency of takeaway meals until you reach a maximum of once a month. Replace takeaway meals with healthier, easy meals prepared at home (see our recipes for alternatives to takeaways on page 239).
- Involve the whole family in planning, preparing or clearing up the evening meal.

Main goal – the meal environment: The whole family will share a relaxed meal together most nights of the week.

Short-term strategies – the meal environment: Use the results from your review to decide what you are aiming for and what you want to change. Here are some examples of environment-related short-term strategies to get you started.

- Switch off the television during meals.
- Eat together as a family, preferably at a table.
- Serve the same meal to each family member.
- Talk and enjoy each other's company, and eat slowly.

> ### Don't forget the vegetables
>
> Dinner is the perfect meal in which to boost your child's vegetable intake. Here are some tips:
> - Stir-fry or microwave vegetables to save time.
> - Speed up oven-roasting by partly cooking vegetables in the microwave first.
> - Wash but don't peel appropriate vegetables (such as carrots and cucumbers).
> - Add vegetables to one-pot dishes and grate them into rissoles.
> - Use low-salt frozen or canned vegetables.
> - Involve your child in preparing a salad.

Making the change – the meal

In **Chapter 6: Making good food available at home**, we set out clear steps to help you plan a weekly menu and prepare a shopping list. These steps are a good place to start when making changes to the evening meals you offer at home. Below are some extra tips to prepare nutritious evening meals – whether you have hours or minutes to get dinner on the table. **Making the change – the meal environment** later in this chapter will help you get the most out of your time together as a family during the evening meal.

1. Write a list of nutritious meals your family enjoys and then use it to plan a weekly dinner menu or have a monthly rotating menu. (See the weekly menu plan on page 45.) Try some of the recipes in this book for new inspiration. Remember, though, that you can revive old family favourites and give them a healthy makeover by using the healthy cooking tips on page 115.

2. Match meals with family activities: do you need quick meals for the nights you have to work late or your child has sports practice after school?

3. Avoid catering to individual likes and dislikes. Provide one option that the majority of your family enjoys. Set a family expectation that everyone will at least try the meal.

Making it easier – the meal

Consider the following tips to help your child embrace healthy dinners.

Prepare meals in advance

Can you prepare tomorrow's dinner tonight after your child has gone to bed? Can you do some preparation in the morning, such as marinating meat or defrosting a frozen dish? Make a few slow-cooked dishes on the weekend: casseroles, curries, hearty soups and pastas are perfect for reheating during the week (see our recipes for slow-cooked meals and soups in **Part 3**). Even better – double or triple the quantity and freeze in batches.

Use a dish in many ways

Make a large batch of bolognese sauce (see recipe on page 232) to use a few times during the week – serve it with pasta, in a lasagne, on a jacket potato and in Mexican wraps or toasted sandwiches. Diced leftover roast meat can be used in a curry, stir-fry or risotto, as a filling for Greek-style wraps or in a hearty salad or soup.

Save quick meals for the busy nights

Minimum effort can still mean maximum nutrition. When you don't have the time or energy to cook, try these quick, balanced meal ideas (see also our recipes for almost-instant meals in **Part 3**):

- Eggs: scrambled or poached eggs on toast, omelettes
- Finger food: on warm nights try chicken and salad rolls or sandwiches; on cool nights serve toasted sandwiches filled with baked beans, tomato and egg, cheese and ham, or tuna, corn and mayonnaise
- Salad: toss together some typical salad ingredients and boost it with boiled egg, tuna or canned legumes such as chickpeas or cannellini beans and then sprinkle with olive oil and vinegar dressing and serve with a slice of wholegrain bread
- Barbecued marinated meat or fish with oven-baked chips or salad

Share cooking with the family

Getting everybody involved can make preparing the evening meal less of a chore, and it's a great opportunity to teach your child about cooking. Preschool children need supervision, and they learn through observation. They can help by collecting ingredients, adding a herb or spice, mixing and mashing, and tasting. During primary school and into adolescence, children need less supervision. They may like some independence and the chance to learn by trial and error. They can build up to taking responsibility for preparing the meal one night a week. Helping can also include setting and clearing the table, washing up and stacking/unstacking the dishwasher.

Do two things at once

Some meals are better suited to multi-tasking. Try these meal ideas when you need to prepare dinner

and help with homework, put on a load of washing or call a friend. Setting an oven timer will remind you to come back to the cooking dinner before anything burns!

- Oven-roasted meat or fish with vegetables
- 'Cheat's risotto', where you add all the stock at once and simmer slowly (this also works well in a rice cooker)
- Soup
- Oven-baked casseroles

Tips for takeaway

Use fast food as your back-up, not your first choice. Plan a week's meals and stick to the shopping list to avoid running out of food towards the end of the week. If you do have a regular takeaway meal, schedule it for once a fortnight or month rather than every week, and choose healthier options from the menu. See the examples over the page.

Tips for dining out

Dining out with your family is a fun occasion, but it doesn't mean you have to leave your healthy eating plans at home! Avoid smorgasbords and meal deals that encourage eating more food than you need; it's easy to over-order and then eat everything on your plate. Why not order several dishes (fewer dishes than people) and put them in the centre of the table so everyone can help themselves? Kids' menus tend to be portions for primary-school-aged children and can be high in kilojoules, saturated fat, salt and sugar. Rather than choosing these options, order a regular meal (such as a bowl of pasta) for yourself and share it with your child. Order a green salad instead of chips; stick to plain bread rather than garlic bread.

Choose water or artificially sweetened drinks rather than sugary drinks. If the meals turn out to be larger than you would normally eat at home, put some aside and request a takeaway bag.

Making the change – the meal environment

Dinner doesn't need to be a big event; it can simply be the expectation that you eat together if you are home at mealtimes. Here are some strategies to make dinner an enjoyable experience for everybody.

1. Set a mealtime so everyone knows when to be at the table. This is particularly useful for teenagers who have to manage their homework and after-school activities. Children can be tired (and/or very hungry) by the time dinner is served, so aim for a dinner time that suits your child's age. An early dinner can help children wind down for the night and avoid hunger-related grumpiness.

2. Encourage your child to talk and listen. Think of conversation topics that move beyond the standard, 'How was school?' Don't overdo it – there's no need to analyse every detail of the day. Try to avoid giving orders – 'Eat your vegetables' – or managing logistics – 'No, you can't go out on the weekend' – at the dinner table. Instead get each member of the family to share something funny they saw or heard that day; ask your child about their friends or their favourite book or song, or discuss your next family outing. Try to leave problems or discipline issues for another time.

3. Encourage your child to eat slowly and enjoy their meal. You can do this by talking about the meal itself and the fun of food – growing

Takeaway type	Main meal	Accompaniment	Hold the soft drinks and . . .
Chicken shop	Barbecued chicken	Green salad and bean salad	Stick to the minimum quantity of chips to share
Italian	Tomato-based pasta sauces	Garden salad	Skip garlic bread and creamy sauces
	Thin-crust pizza	Vegetarian toppings	Skip salami, extra cheese and extra meat
Indian	Tandoori meat or tomato-based sauce with vegetables	Steamed rice	Avoid pappadams, samosas, coconut-milk-based sauces
Fish and chip shop	Grilled fish	Peas, corn or salad	Stick to the minimum quantity of chips to share
	Hamburger, steak sandwich	Extra salad	Skip cheese, egg and bacon, chips
Greek	Yiros or kebabs	Extra salad	Avoid creamy garlic sauces
Chinese	Beef or chicken and vegetable stir-fry	Steamed rice, steamed dim sim	Skip fried rice, spring rolls, dim sims
Thai	Tom yum soup	Steamed rice, cold rolls	Avoid spring rolls, laksa and other coconut-milk-based dishes

it, colours, textures, how it can be prepared. Ask how they might prepare it differently.

4. Minimise distractions by switching off the television and mobile phones, and banning toys and books from the dinner table.

5. Let meals come to a natural end; aim for around 20–30 minutes. A family rule that you stay at the table until all family members have finished eating provides a chance for your child to enjoy the social side of eating.

Making it easier – the meal environment

Consider the following tips to help your child enjoy the family-dinner experience.

Avoid food bribes

Offering dessert to get your child to finish their vegetables seems effective when you are busy, tired or frustrated, but in the long term bribes, rewards or threats can actually make your child dislike the things you were trying to encourage. Setting a good example and offering praise ('Well done for trying the zucchini tonight' or 'I really enjoyed our family dinner chat tonight') are better approaches. Even though they don't offer the quick fix quite like a food reward, they will have a better long-term result. (See also **Food rewards and bribes** on page 47.)

Don't force your child to finish everything on their plate if they are full

Phrases like, 'Good girl for eating everything' are not helpful because they teach your child to clean their plate or continue to eat when they are full.

Tricky situations

Following are some common scenarios, and ideas for managing them. Aim to use 'Take 2' examples with your child (see box on page 98).

Managing the influence of family and friends

Talk to your extended family and friends about what you are trying to achieve, particularly if your child spends time in their homes during meal and snack times. You might inspire them to come along for the ride with you, in which case you can share some of the strategies you are trying. Consider setting a rule with your child so they ask you whether they can have a food that is offered to them.

Teens and the evening meal

As teenagers become more independent and socially active they tend to be home for fewer evening meals. When they are home, think of dinner as a chance to sit down together rather than pressuring them to talk about serious issues. Take advantage of their emerging independence and opinions by asking them to help plan and prepare evening meals for the family. If your teen has a part-time job that clashes with dinner time, keep leftovers in single portions they can eat at work or when they get home. When they are out socialising, they can still choose healthy options. Their budget will influence their choices, so give them some ideas for healthier choices that don't break the bank. They can buy water rather than sugary drinks and downsize the portion of chips, or not buy them at all. Also suggest filling alternatives to burgers, such as baked potatoes, sushi or stir-fried vegetables with steamed rice.

Scenario	Take 1 – common responses, but try to avoid these	Take 2 – better responses to use instead
'I don't want this for dinner!'	'Okay, what do you want me to make you instead?'	'This is what is available tonight. You have eaten it before.' Or 'There is (*a preferred food*) on your plate, you can eat that. But I would still like you to taste a little bit of everything.'
'I'm not hungry!'	'But you need to eat!'	'Okay, well the next meal is breakfast; can you get through until then?' Remind them that the next eating occasion won't be until the morning (not dessert!). After those gentle prompts, take the leftover food away without a fuss. If they consistently leave leftovers, consider serving a smaller meal.
'I don't like it!'	'If you eat it you can have dessert.'	'Yes, it's something new. But I think you will like it as much as I do.' Encourage a taste.
'I'm still hungry!'	'That's no good; what else would you like?'	'Why don't you wait for 10 minutes to see if you fill up? There is vegetables/salad or a piece of fruit if you are still hungry then.'
'I'm finished first!'	'Aren't you a good fast eater!'	'Eating isn't a race. Remember to chew your food lots of times and enjoy every mouthful.'

Parenting tips for making evening meals easier

 Modelling Share family meals, and talk about food or cooking together. Eat the same meal as your child at dinner time.

 Monitoring Keep your eyes on the plate! Be aware of how often vegetables feature in the evening meals you offer. Take note of the ways your family commitments and work influence your evening meals.

 Setting boundaries Ensure everyone is clear on family meal rules, such as asking before taking food at social occasions or being ready for a set dinner time.

 Reinforce the positive Focus on the journey as well as the destination. If your child tries a new vegetable, praise them!

 Managing resistance Don't provide an alternative meal if your child dislikes something; they will learn to accept what is offered or wait until breakfast.

Related information
See **Chapter 10: Phasing out sweet drinks** for more on drinks offered at mealtime. **Chapter 6: Making good food available at home**, the tools in **Part 4** and the recipes in **Part 3** contain lots of useful tips relevant to the evening meal.

reducing screen time

Children have so many options when it comes to sceen-based entertainment – television, game consoles, mobile phones, computers and the Internet – but with your encouragement, they can have just as much fun playing non-screen games, sport and other activities.

Setting the scene

When it's too hot or too cold to be outside (or when you just need something to entertain your child), many of us appreciate how well the television, console games and computers occupy children. You may wonder why you need to worry about a little television and a few computer games – isn't this electronic wizardry educational for children? Yes, it can be, but there is a downside to a lifestyle that involves too much screen-based entertainment.

This type of entertainment entices your child to sit still for long periods of time, which can increase the risk of developing cardiovascular disease and diabetes, regardless of how active they are at other times. It can also trigger snacking (particularly 'sometimes' foods), expose your child to unrealistic body images, discourage activity and outdoor play, interfere with sleep patterns and set viewing habits that continue into adulthood.

In this chapter we provide strategies, skills and tools to reduce your family's screen time so it is more evenly balanced with being active, socialising, completing homework and fulfilling family responsibilities.

Where do I start?

You need to get a clear idea of your family's screen use. Use the screen-time log below to monitor usage for one week. Start with the television, then consider computers and game consoles, and combine the information to get a clear picture of the whole week. (Don't include the time your child spends doing homework on the computer.) It is also worth making a note of what you are doing while your child watches television or plays computer games. You might want to do this separately for each family member. (Older

Child's name:	Television (+ DVDs, videos)	Computer (Internet, computer games)	Game consoles	Parent was doing . . .	Daily total
Monday					
Tuesday					
Wednesday					
Thursday					
Friday					
Saturday					
Sunday					
				Weekly total	

children can log their own screen use.) Keep the log sheet in a common place, such as on the fridge or next to the television, as a reminder to fill it in. Also look at how much television you watch and whether it is on in the background.

Once you have logged the family's screen time for a week, calculate the screen use of each individual and compare it to the guidelines: no more than 2 hours a day, particularly during daylight hours, or for children aged 2–5, less than 1 hour a day. Television is not recommended at all for children under 2 years.

> ## Think beyond screen time
> Being a couch potato or 'sitting' for long periods of time can affect our health regardless of how active we are. Depending on your child's age, sitting might include being in a pram, sitting while reading, playing computer games or text-messaging. Limit sedentary or 'sitting' time as much as possible and encourage children to take every opportunity to crawl, play, move, walk and be active.

What should I aim for?

Main goal: My child will spend no more than 2 hours a day on recreational screen activities.

Short-term strategies:

Use the results from your screen-time log to decide what you are aiming for and what you want to change. Here are some examples to get you started.

- Gradually reduce the family's screen use by 15 minutes a day until you watch fewer than 2 hours a day.
- Remove televisions from bedrooms.

- Have two screen-free days a week.
- Keep the television switched off until all homework is completed.
- Limit Internet surfing to 30 minutes per person per day.
- Keep 'screens' switched off at mealtimes. Gradually extend this rule to include before school, during homework time (except when the computer is required for homework), during wind-down time before bed, during daylight hours and then during the school week.
- Have a one-week 'no TV' challenge.

Making the change

Reducing your family's screen time will support many other changes, such as finding more time to be active, preparing healthy meals and encouraging earlier bedtimes. Here are some tips to get you started.

1. Involve your child in setting your goals. Explain why you are making these changes. Keep the reasons simple and relevant – such as having more time to practise their favourite sport, socialise with friends or play after school.

2. At the beginning of each week use a television guide to plan your child's weekly viewing. Are there any programs your child particularly likes to watch? Ask them to nominate their favourites, providing the amount of time does not exceed their daily allowance – this will help them stick to the screen rules but still see their favourite programs. Remember that the amount of television *and* other screen-based entertainment should not exceed 2 hours.

3. Establish a rule that younger children need to ask your permission to turn on the television or other screens.

4. Make sure the television is turned off after the end of scheduled shows – using a timer with a buzzer might be a fun reminder for your children to stick to the rules.

Making it easier

Consider the following tips to help your child stick to their daily allowance of recreational screen time.

Make the most of daylight hours

If your child's favourite television show is screened when it's still light outside, consider recording it. Your child can then be active outside (or finish homework or complete their chores) before the sun sets. They can watch the show later and fast-forward the ads, reducing their overall viewing time.

Share the space

The fewer screens you have in your home, the more your child will use them. Make a family rule that all bedrooms (including yours) are screen-free zones. It's easier to monitor what your child is watching or doing when the television and computer are in shared rooms such as the living room. This is especially useful for monitoring Internet content.

Combating boredom

How many times have you heard, 'I'm bored! Can I watch TV?' There's no doubt your child will try to slip back into their old screen habits. Be prepared to stand firm, and have lots of alternative ideas up your sleeve. Encourage them to do something active – help them make a list of after-school activities to remind them of all the things they enjoy other than watching television – and if they can't find anything to do suggest they finish their homework, help with chores or get organised for the next day.

Praise and rewards

Don't forget to praise your child when they do the right thing. Use words that remind them of the good behaviour, such as, 'I really liked the way you played outside together straight after school today.' Avoid using sedentary time, such as extra TV time, as a reward.

Tricky situations
Teenagers and screen use

You might find parenting increasingly challenging as your child grows into a teenager, and changing viewing habits might be tough. One way to approach this subject is to focus on time management. Help your teen plan what they do after school. Timetabling when everything gets done – homework, sports practice, a part-time job – might highlight how little time they have for screen-based entertainment.

Another way to tap into their desire for independence – and cut down opportunities for sitting in front of the screen – is to increase their responsibilities at home. For example, suggest they cook dinner one night a week. This will leave them with less time for Internet surfing while also teaching them important life skills.

It's not all about avoiding the screen, though. If television gives you and your teenager the opportunity to bond and interact, plan your viewing together so it is still within the daily 2-hour limit.

Not at home to monitor screen use?

This is a common problem for working parents. Try writing a list of things your child should do before you get home: finishing homework, taking the dog for a walk, setting the table for dinner, even preparing dinner if you have older children.

What do I do when they just won't turn off?

Consequences! Consequences! Consequences! Are they clear and understood? Do you follow through with them?

Parenting tips for reducing screen time

 Modelling Show your child other ways to relax or socialise by switching some of your own screen time with other activities, such as cooking, gardening, reading and playing non-screen games.

 Monitoring Keep track of how much screen time family members build up, including time spent watching television, playing computer games and surfing the Internet.

 Setting boundaries Establish family rules to keep screen time to a maximum of 2 hours per day.

 Encouraging desirable behaviour Help your child plan their viewing time by making an after-school activities list to remind them of all the things they enjoy other than watching television.

 Managing resistance Be consistent and stand your ground: if your child has agreed to turn the television off after a particular show has finished, ensure this happens.

> **Related information**
> See **Chapter 3: Leading an active lifestyle** and **Chapter 15: Becoming an active family**.

becoming an active family

Modelling a healthy, active lifestyle will encourage your child to value physical activity and establish habits to see them through life.

Setting the scene

Being active is an important part of your child's physical and emotional development – and a great way to have fun. Unfortunately we find many reasons for being inactive – 'We're too busy' is the most common. While this can be true, it also reflects the low value our society tends to place on physical activity. Your attitudes about physical activity have a strong influence on your child. Think about the activity you do each day. Do you take the lift instead of the stairs? Do you leave the car at home and walk or cycle? Do you cancel outdoor activities at the first sign of rain? Do you think of activity as an opportunity, or is it a drag? Your child absorbs these subtle messages and will probably follow in your footsteps.

In this chapter we provide strategies and tools to get your family moving and embracing an active lifestyle – for life.

Are you really too busy to be active?

The most common reason people give for inactivity is being 'too busy'. Let's dig a little deeper. We know that on a school day the average Australian child spends 2 hours watching television and another hour on other screen-based entertainment; on weekends and holidays they spend an average of 3 hours watching television and another 1.5 hours on other screen-based entertainment. So if your family struggles to be active, it might be worth reviewing your television viewing habits.

Where do I start?

You need to get a clear idea of the amount and type of physical activity your child undertakes each week. Many parents believe that their children get enough physical activity at school or childcare, but this isn't always the case. Do you really know how active your child is? The sample chart below shows you how to record their activity for a week. You might need to ask your child, their carer or coach how long your child did a certain activity, if you weren't there.

Activity table	Before school/ morning	During school/ daytime	After school/ afternoon	Evening	Total
Monday		PE class (35 minutes)			35 minutes
Tuesday			Soccer practice (40 minutes)		40 minutes
Wednesday	Ride to school (15 minutes)	Handball at recess and lunch (15+20 minutes)	Ride home (10 minutes)		1 hour
Thursday				Rostered night to walk the dog (45 minutes)	45 minutes
Friday		PE class (35 minutes)			35 minutes
Saturday	Soccer (40 minutes)		Mucking about with friends outside (60 minutes)		1 hour, 40 minutes
Sunday					0 minutes

What should I aim for?

Main goal: The whole family will accumulate at least 60 minutes of moderate to vigorous physical activity every day. Children under 5 will have several hours of active play each day.

Short-term strategies:

Use the results from your review of your child's activity levels to decide what you are aiming for and what you want to change. Your short-term strategies might be to increase the time spent in one or more activity your child already does or to take up a new activity. If your family isn't very active make sure you set realistic goals – remember that any amount of extra activity is an improvement. Start slowly and then gradually build up to longer, more frequent sessions.

Here are some examples of different kinds of activity opportunities. Use a mixture to get children active.

- Unstructured activity: Play that comes naturally to children. Play can be alone or with friends, for example, playing in the park, walking or riding a bike, surfing, skateboarding or general household duties such as vacuuming or gardening. Equipment such as skipping ropes and totem tennis are great when they don't have someone else to play with. Get to know the facilities available near you (parks and ovals, tracks and trails, beaches, skate parks and swimming pools).
- Structured activity: Usually organised and may involve rules or a goal of some sort, such as school sport classes, swimming or dancing lessons. You could encourage your child to take up a sport or activity they show interest in, such as scouts, guides, athletics or dance classes. Check with your council for local activities.
- Organised sport: Team or individual sports that involve rules and are generally competitive, such as football, soccer, basketball, netball or athletics. You could encourage your child to try a school or club sport that trains or plays games during after-school hours. Choose something that is right for your child's age and ability.
- Active transport: Choosing an active way to get to and from a place, such as walking, cycling or skateboarding to school, the park or the local shops. You may want to get a bag rack for their bike. If the distance is too far, try driving part of the way and then walking the rest, or walk or ride in one direction each day. Slowly build this up to help reach the minimum 60 minutes of activity each day.
- Active family activities: Take active family outings regularly (weekly or fortnightly). Go to the beach or local pool, walk or have a picnic in a park or garden, or take a family bike ride. Spend 15 minutes playing a bat-and-ball game or any active game with your child several times each week and then build up to longer sessions. If you find it difficult to spend a block of time with your child, shorter, more frequent time can be just as effective. You could get a game started (such as totem tennis), leave them to it, and pop in regularly to keep it going.
- School-holiday activities: During school holidays encourage your child to be active by providing equipment, transporting and supervising them at parks, skate parks

and bike tracks, and encouraging visits with friends.

- Outside after-school play: Encourage your child to spend 30 minutes or more playing outside after school. Some ideas include handball in the driveway or on a deck, trampolines, swings, sandpit, flying a kite together, jumps for bikes in the driveway, and water balloons.

Making the change

Getting your child to be more active requires a whole family commitment. Here is a step-by-step plan to get you started.

1. Plan activity times using the activity table on page 106.

2. Use the activity table to work out the times when there are opportunities for your family to be active.

3. Talk to your child about the activities they enjoy doing and why. In what ways would they like to be active? Would they like to go to the park more often, or try a new sport? Would having friends over more frequently encourage extra activity? Asking for your child's thoughts might produce some unexpected answers. For example, your teenager might not want to be active at recess and lunchtime like they were in primary school; they may worry about sweat or body odour, they might need more supportive underwear, or they may simply think it isn't a cool thing to do with their friends. In this case this information can help you offer suitable

alternatives to get your child moving after school and on weekends.

4. Together, brainstorm some activity options. Consider the different types of activities so that there are options to suit different opportunities identified in the activity table. Enjoyment is fundamental to your child being and remaining active, so let your child choose the activity or bear this in mind when you are offering suggestions.

Making it easier

Consider the following tips to help your child embrace an active lifestyle.

Get involved

Think about how you can be more active as this is one of the most effective ways to help your child become more active. Getting an activity started or supporting from the sidelines is also important when you can't actively participate. It shows that you support their active pastime and helps reinforce that you value being active.

Be prepared

When your child asks the inevitable question, 'I'm bored, can I watch television?' be prepared with some fun, active alternatives. After-school activities might include riding or walking home from school, going to a local park, inviting friends over to play or trying a sport that involves after-school practice. For activities in the backyard, keep a box of equipment appropriate for their age at your back door – include bats, balls, racquets, skipping ropes, hula-hoops, Frisbee, a net, yoyos, string, chalk, cones and toys – and encourage your child and their friends to rummage and be creative in the ways they use the equipment. Keep some equipment – balls or a Frisbee – in the boot of the car so that you can make the most of opportunities when you are out and about.

Don't let the weather stop you

On a rainy day put your raincoats on and head outdoors anyway. It's okay to get wet – just make sure kids are warm and dry when they return indoors. Use the carport or undercover outdoor area to play in or try indoor swimming, indoor cricket, indoor rock climbing, ice-skating, or even window shopping at your local shopping centre. If your outdoor options are limited, clear a play area indoors and try balloon games, 'Simon Says', dancing to music, musical chairs, dress-ups, hide and seek, indoor bowls, building an indoor cubby house, performing a concert or playing board games. It might even be a chance to ask your child to clean and reorganise their bedroom.

Make it safe

Part of the fun of being active is trying new things, and inevitably this will cause some falls, bruises and scratches, maybe even a broken bone. Remind yourself that negotiating risk is an important part of growing up. There are simple ways you can help ensure that your child plays safely: provide a safe area and supervise while they play; set (and consistently apply) rules about appropriate protective clothing (helmets, knee and elbow pads, a hat when outdoors); and educate your child about road safety, how to be wary of strangers, and necessary information such as their full name, address and phone number. For older children, supervision may change. You need to know where they are, whom they are with and when to expect them home. They should always be with friends or siblings if they are playing unsupervised. Take it in turns with other parents or neighbours to supervise after school and on weekends.

Gifts that promote being active

Use occasions such as birthdays and Christmas to give your child equipment or games that promote activity rather than a games console or computer games.

Organised sport – is it the best option?

Organised sport may not necessarily be preferred by every child. If it is too competitive, it may result in negative experiences, particularly if your child is just starting to be active, has not yet gained confidence in their ability or is overweight and concerned about how they look. But overall, competition can help children learn to win or lose

Make school holidays active

Holidays are not a time to slouch in front of the television. Stick to your family's rules about screen use (see **Chapter 14: Reducing screen time**) and encourage your child to use this extra time to be active and try new things.

Tricky situations
Keeping your teenager active

When your child hits their teenage years their activity levels tend to decrease, so it is vital that you continue to encourage an active lifestyle. This can be difficult, because you don't have control over their activity level and they don't need you as a playmate any more. But your role as a parent, encouraging and supporting your child to be active, never stops.

Your child's preferences might change too, so take the time to find out what they want to try. Think beyond traditional sports – what will they enjoy doing with their friends? Cycling, kickboxing, dancing, bocce, yoga, sailing, tae kwon do or gym classes?

Adolescent girls and activity

Adolescent girls are even less active than boys and younger children. It can be a developmentally intense time when issues such as self-esteem and body image impact their activity levels. At this stage, special attention and support from mothers can be particularly effective in encouraging teenage

graciously – that's part of life! Be sure to encourage your child's effort rather than the outcome. Look for supportive clubs that are inclusive of all abilities. Keep it fun – your child is more likely to get involved in activities if they are having fun, so let them choose the activity and lead the play. Suggest activities that suit their age and level of development and offer praise to boost their confidence.

girls to stay active. Think about what might motivate your daughter to be more active. Sometimes it is the social aspect that is most appealing, so highlight this. Lead by example and show your daughter that an active lifestyle is a lifelong habit.

What if my child is just not interested in being active?

Talk to your child about why they are not interested. For many, a lack of confidence holds them back. If this is the case, provide plenty of praise and encouragement, and spend time being active with your child to help develop their skills and confidence. As these grow, talk to your child about joining a team or enrolling in classes. Ensure your child has the necessary equipment to participate comfortably. Does your daughter have a supportive, properly fitted bra? Is your child concerned about sweating and body odour? (They might want to try a different antiperspirant deodorant.) Are their sports shoes comfortable? Do they have the correct uniform? Create opportunities for them to be active in small groups they feel comfortable with and suggest active ways to 'hang out' (such as ten-pin bowling or window shopping).

Parenting tips for becoming an active family

 Modelling Let your child see you leading and enjoying an active lifestyle.

 Monitoring Keep a check on all the everyday opportunities to be active as a family: taking the stairs, parking further away from the shops, walking the last 10 minutes to school. It all adds up.

 Setting boundaries Set a family rule that some of after-school time is outdoor-play time.

 Encouraging desirable behaviour Make time to be active as a family, or watch and praise your child as they play. This is just as important when they play in the backyard as it is when they are on the sports field.

 Managing resistance Encourage your child to try different sports, games or ways to be active. They may need to try a range of activities before they find something they enjoy.

> **Related information**
>
> **Chapter 3: Leading an active lifestyle** provides information on how active children should be.
>
> **Chapter 14: Reducing screen time** will help your child create more time in their day to be active.

recipes

healthy cooking

When preparing food there are some very basic things you can do to make it healthier. Try these simple ideas when choosing recipes and preparing meals and snacks.

Reduce saturated fat

- Replace full-fat dairy products with fat-reduced options.
- Replace cream with fat-reduced evaporated milk.
- Replace sour cream with fat-reduced yoghurt.
- Replace butter with oil or margarine.
- Replace coconut milk or cream with fat-reduced or light options, and use sparingly.
- Replace regular pastry with fat-reduced or filo pastry.
- Remove visible fat and skin from meat or poultry before cooking.
- Use cooking methods such as grilling, pan-frying, stir-frying, barbecuing, poaching, steaming, roasting and baking, and avoid frequent deep-frying.
- Choose lean minced meat as an inexpensive ingredient for quick meals.

Reduce salt

- Flavour with spices and herbs rather than salt and stock cubes.
- Don't add salt when cooking and don't put salt on the table.

- Limit fish/soy/oyster sauces to 1–2 tablespoons per recipe and use salt-reduced varieties.
- Use salt-reduced canned or frozen vegetables.
- Use salt-reduced stock; use half the required quantity of stock powder or substitute half the liquid stock for water.

Increase fibre

- Add legumes to casseroles, pasta sauces, salads and soups.
- Use wholegrain breads, crispbreads, rolls and breakfast cereals.
- Use half wholemeal and half white flour when baking.
- Try brown rice and wholemeal pasta for variety.

Increase vegetables

- Serve a variety of coloured vegetables with lunch and dinner.
- Add extra vegetables to casseroles, soups, pasta sauces and curries.
- Serve a mug of vegetable soup as an entree or after-school snack.
- Serve a side salad to meals that don't contain enough vegetables.
- Avoid peeling vegetables where possible (see **Risk of choking** for exceptions); always wash them thoroughly.

Risk of choking

Children under 4 can be at risk of choking as they are still learning to eat and do not have back teeth to chew and grind food. Supervise children as they eat (while sitting down). Cut meat into small pieces and remove skin and fat. Grate, cook or mash hard fruits and vegetables (such as carrot, celery and apple). Remove the skin and halve grapes; pit cherries. Avoid nuts, popcorn, corn chips and hard, sticky lollies.

food and shopping guide

There are so many products on supermarket shelves, and a number of factors to consider when choosing food. The nutritional considerations for one type of food (such as the fibre content of bread) will be different from another food type (such as the fat content of yoghurt).

To make shopping easier and faster:

- Use a shopping list based on your weekly meal plan.
- Prioritise foods from the basic food groups and minimise the number of 'sometimes' foods (see page 24) in your shopping trolley.
- If you can't decide between similar products, one labelled with the Heart Foundation Tick (see page 119) will represent a healthier choice.
- Use this shopping guide to make healthy food choices and get around the supermarket aisles faster.

Fruit and vegetables

Fresh fruit and vegetables: Choose seasonal where possible, for best quality, flavour and value for money.

Canned fruit and vegetables: Choose products with no added (or low) salt and sugar.

Canned fruit: Choose those in natural juice.

Frozen potato products: Choose products with the Heart Foundation Tick.

Frozen vegetables: Avoid those that contain 'flavour sachets', which can be high in salt.

Meat, poultry and and fish

Meat and poultry: Choose the leanest cuts that fit your budget. Consider the relative weight of the bone when working out value for money.

Canned salmon and tuna: Choose those in spring water.

Frozen fish products: Choose products with the Heart Foundation Tick.

Legumes

Canned legumes: Choose products with no added salt, where possible.

Bread and cereals

Bread: Choose wholegrain, wholemeal, rye or high-fibre white bread. Also try wholegrain or wholemeal English muffins, crumpets, Turkish, pita or burritos.

Rice: Choose a mixture of brown, Arborio, Dongara or basmati, along with white varieties.

Pasta: Choose a mixture of wholemeal and white.

Noodles: Choose fresh and dried, white or wholemeal.

Other grains and cereals: Try couscous, polenta, pearl barley or burghul (cracked wheat).

Flour: Choose a mixture of white and wholemeal.

Fat-reduced dairy

Milk: Choose fat-reduced (less than 2 per cent fat) milk for yourself and children aged over 2 years. Fat-reduced UHT (long-life) milk and skim milk powder are convenient, inexpensive alternatives with similar nutritional value.

Evaporated milk: Choose fat-reduced.

Buttermilk: Choose fat-reduced.

Yoghurt: Choose fat-reduced yoghurt for yourself and children aged over 2.

Custard: Choose fat-reduced or buy custard powder and mix it with fat-reduced milk.

Cheese: Choose fat-reduced cheese, including parmesan.

Soft cheese (cottage, ricotta, cream): Choose fat-reduced, and remember that these cheeses have less calcium than hard cheese.

Soy and other products: Choose calcium-fortified, fat-reduced products.

Healthy fats and oils

Margarine: Choose low-salt, polyunsaturated or monounsaturated margarines. Avoid dairy blends and table margarines because they can be high in saturated fat.

Oil: Choose vegetable oils such as canola, olive, safflower, sunflower or corn. Avoid palm oil and coconut oil (also sold as Copha) because these are high in saturated fat.

Condiments

Spices and fresh or dried herbs: Try pepper, caraway seeds, cinnamon, curry powder, garam masala, cumin, nutmeg, paprika, ginger, garlic, parsley, basil, mint, coriander, thyme, oregano, tarragon, bay leaves, rosemary, and so on.

Seasonings and stocks: Choose salt-reduced.

Tomato sauce and tomato paste: Choose salt-reduced.

Spreads for sandwiches: Try pesto, tomato salsa, pickles, chutney, apple sauce, fat-reduced mayonnaise.

Asian sauces: Choose salt-reduced or light soy sauce, plum sauce, sweet chilli sauce, sesame oil, fish sauce, kecap manis, oyster sauce, hoisin sauce.

Flavours for meat marinades: Try barbecue sauce, tandoori paste, mint sauce.

Simple salad dressing ingredients: Choose dressings based on lemon juice, balsamic vinegar, mustard and oil.

Canned foods

Baked beans and spaghetti: Choose salt-reduced.

Soup: Choose salt-reduced vegetable-based soups; avoid cream-based soups and products containing coconut milk or cream.

Drinks

Water: Tap water is the best choice because it contains fluoride in most parts of Australia.

Flavoured milk: Choose fat-reduced.

Juice: Choose unsweetened varieties and small-portion packs. Avoid fruit-juice drinks.

Cordial: Choose artificially sweetened.

Soft drinks: Choose plain mineral or soda water, or artificially sweetened options.

Fruit-flavoured fizzy drinks: Choose artificially sweetened.

Breakfast cereals

Choose high-fibre, low-sugar and low-salt varieties such as Weet-Bix, Weeties, natural untoasted muesli and oats or porridge.

Crispbreads and crackers

Choose wholegrain products that are low in salt or those with the Heart Foundation Tick, which have met strict standards for salt and fibre.

The Heart Foundation Tick

The Heart Foundation Tick was developed to help consumers identify healthier products. Foods that carry the Tick are randomly tested to ensure they meet the Heart Foundation's strict standards to limit the amount of kilojoules, saturated fat, salt and trans fats in foods, and they must also offer some 'good' nutrients, such as fibre, calcium or protein. When you are faced with several varieties of a product on the supermarket shelf, the Tick will help you identify the healthier options for all the food categories listed here.

good food that your kids will love

Food needs to provide us with the nourishment we require to live, work and play. But no one wants to eat a meal that is simply good for them – it must taste great and look appealing too. And for busy families, quick meals or recipes that work with our schedules are another all-important factor. In the recipes that follow, we aim to meet all these needs. Here we have done the hard work for you: devising nutritionally sound dishes that are also down-right delicious.

Keep in mind that each recipe in this book offers a foundation you can build on or adapt to your own family's needs. If a member of your family has a dairy allergy, for instance, omit the cheese or switch from cow's milk to your preferred alternative. If you don't have a particular herb, spice or vegetable to hand, try replacing it with something you to have in your fridge or pantry. The number of serves each recipe makes is a guide only. The quantity a toddler eats will obviously be less than what a teenager would eat, so you may need to double quantities (or keep leftovers) depending on your family's needs and size. So use these recipes as inspiration, but have the confidence to adapt to your family's needs.

breakfast

healthy breakfast suggestions

A healthy breakfast doesn't have to take a lot of effort to prepare. Be inspired by the suggestions pictured here or try some of the recipe ideas that follow.

Little ones' muesli

Little ones' muesli
Makes 450 g

2 cups rolled oats
¼ cup pepitas
1 tablespoon sesame seeds
¼ cup sunflower seeds
2 tablespoons honey
½ cup apple juice
1 cup rice puffs
1 cup bran flakes
½ cup sultanas
½ cup dried apricots (or other
    dried fruit), sliced

Preheat the oven to 180°C. Place the oats, pepitas, sesame seeds and sunflower seeds in a large bowl. Pour the honey and juice over the oats and stir well to combine. Transfer the mixture to a baking tray and bake for 20–25 minutes until golden. Remove from the oven and cool completely. Stir in the rice puffs, bran flakes, sultanas and apricots. Store in an airtight container.

✱ Toasting the oats and seeds in honey and apple juice is optional. If skipping this step, omit the juice and honey.

✱ Pepita seeds are not suitable for children under the age of 4 years due to the risk of choking.

✱ Omit the seeds if there is a nut or seed allergy in the family.

Bircher muesli
Serves 4

2 cups rolled oats
¼ cup almond meal (optional)
1 apple, grated
¼ cup sultanas
2 cups fat-reduced milk
200 g fat-reduced vanilla yoghurt
seasonal fruit, to serve

Soak the oats, almond meal, apple and sultanas in the milk and keep in the fridge overnight. Stir in the yoghurt just before serving. Top with seasonal fruit, such as strawberries, sliced banana, kiwi fruit or plums.

✱ Store, covered, in the fridge for 2 days.

✱ Omit the almond meal if there is a nut allergy in the family

Fruity breakfast blocks
Serves 2

4 wheat breakfast biscuits
   (such as Weet-Bix or Vita Brits)
2 tablespoons sultanas
2 tablespoons finely chopped dried apple
2 tablespoons flaked almonds,
   lightly toasted (optional)
fat-reduced milk, to serve

Lightly crush the wheat biscuits into two serving bowls and sprinkle the fruit and nuts over the top. Serve with fat-reduced milk.

✳ Nuts are not suitable for children under the age of 4 years due to the risk of choking.

✳ Omit the almonds if there is a nut allergy in the family.

Crunchy munchy muesli
Makes 350 g

1 cup rolled oats
1 cup bran flakes
1 cup corn flakes
1 cup rice puffs
¼ cup finely sliced dried peach
¼ cup currants
¼ cup sunflower seeds
¼ cup skinned hazelnuts or almonds,
   toasted and roughly chopped
fat-reduced yoghurt and milk and fresh fruit,
   to serve

Place all the dry ingredients in a large bowl and stir to combine. Store in an airtight container. Serve with fat-reduced yoghurt and milk as well as fresh fruit.

✳ Experiment with different types of your favourite dried fruits in place of the peach and currants in this recipe.

✳ Nuts are not suitable for children under the age of 4 years due to the risk of choking.

✳ Omit the sunflower seeds or nuts if there is a nut or seed allergy in the family.

Crunchy munchy muesli

Apple porridge

Serves 4

2 cups rolled oats
4 cups fat-reduced milk (or half water, half milk)
1 medium Granny Smith apple, coarsely grated
¼ teaspoon ground cinnamon
1 tablespoon brown sugar (optional)
fat-reduced milk or water, to serve

Place the oats, milk, apple and cinnamon in a heavy-based saucepan over medium heat and bring to the boil, stirring constantly. Reduce the heat and simmer for 5 minutes.

Spoon the porridge into serving dishes. Sprinkle over brown sugar and serve with extra milk.

Variations

Porridge with banana and sultanas
Omit the apple from the above recipe. Stir into the finished porridge a handful of sultanas. Top each bowl of porridge with half a banana, sliced.

Pear and almond porridge
Replace the apple with 1 large firm pear, cored and coarsely grated. Sprinkle over the top of the porridge a handful of slivered almonds.

✱ Nuts are not suitable for children under the age of 4 years due to the risk of choking.

✱ Omit the almonds if there is a nut allergy in the family.

Porridge with ruby red rhubarb
Omit the apple from the above recipe. Serve the finished porridge with a dollop of ruby red rhubarb (see page 138).

Apple porridge

Banana and strawberry smoothie

Banana and strawberry smoothie

Serves 2

1 cup fat-reduced milk
1 ripe banana
6 strawberries, hulled and halved
1 tablespoon honey (optional)
200 g fat-reduced vanilla yoghurt

Place all the ingredients in a blender and whiz until smooth. Pour the smoothies into two tall glasses and serve immediately.

* If you prefer, you can leave out the yoghurt and increase the quantity of milk to 2 cups.

Variations

Banana cinnamon smoothie

Replace the fruit in the above recipe with 2 ripe bananas and ¼ teaspoon ground cinnamon.

Choc-banana smoothie

Replace the fruit in the above recipe with 1 ripe banana and 2 tablespoons drinking chocolate. You don't need to add honey to this combination.

Mixed frozen berry smoothie

Replace the fruit in the above recipe with 250 g frozen berries. In this case use berry yoghurt rather than vanilla yoghurt.

Fuzzy mango peach smoothie

Replace the fruit in the above recipe with 125 g diced and drained canned peaches (in natural juice) and 2 frozen mango cheeks. In this case use peach and mango yoghurt.

* You can store all kinds of leftover chunks of fruit in the freezer to use to make delicious smoothies at a later date. Peel and freeze over-ripe bananas, cheeks of mango, wedges of peach or mandarin, for example.

Tomatoes on toast

The following three meals can be served for breakfast, lunch or as a hearty snack. Increase the quantity of toast to make the meal more substantial.

Tomatoes on toast

Serves 4

1 tablespoon olive oil
4 vine-ripened tomatoes, cut into
  1 cm thick slices
¼ teaspoon dried oregano or
  4 fresh basil leaves, torn
4 slices wholegrain toast

Heat the oil in a medium frying pan over medium heat. Add the tomato slices, sprinkle with oregano and cook for 2 minutes each side until golden and starting to collapse. Serve with wholegrain toast.

Mushrooms on toast

Serves 4

2 tablespoons olive oil
300 g button mushrooms, halved
2 tablespoons roughly chopped
  parsley (optional)
4 slices wholegrain toast

Heat the oil in a medium frying pan over medium heat. Add the mushrooms and cook for 3 minutes until they begin to brown. Add ½ cup water and simmer until the water has evaporated and mushrooms are soft. Stir in the parsley and serve with wholegrain toast.

Baked beans with onion and ham

Serves 4

1 small brown onion, roughly chopped
50 g sliced lean ham
425 g can pureed tomatoes
¼ cup barbecue sauce
2 tablespoons brown sugar (optional)
2 × 400 g cans cannellini beans, drained
  and rinsed
4 slices wholegrain toast

Place the onion and ham in a food processor and whiz until finely chopped. Add the puréed tomatoes, barbecue sauce and brown sugar and whiz until combined. (Alternatively, finely chop the onion and ham, then combine in the saucepan with the puréed tomatoes, sauce and sugar.)

Pour into a medium saucepan and place over medium heat. Bring to the boil, then reduce the heat and simmer for 15 minutes until thick and reduced. Stir in the beans and simmer for a further 10 minutes until heated through. Serve with wholegrain toast.

Summery fruit salad

Cinnamon apple

Ruby-red rhubarb

breakfast fruit toppings

Pink fruit salad

Everyday fruit salad

Spoon these delicious fruit toppings over cereal, use as a sweet finish to a cooked breakfast or spoon into a bowl and serve with fat-reduced yoghurt as a light breakfast. They can also be served with fat-reduced yoghurt or custard for dessert or supper.

Fresh fruit ideas to serve at breakfast

All year round: canned fruit, frozen berries
Summer: stone fruit such as peaches, nectarines and apricots;
    and berries such as strawberries and blueberries; grapes, cherries
Autumn: apples, pears, figs, kiwi fruit
Winter: oranges, mandarins
Spring: papaya, melons, bananas

Cinnamon apple

4 medium green apples, peeled, cored and cut into 2 cm wedges
½ teaspoon ground cinnamon
1 tablespoon brown sugar

Place all the ingredients and 2 tablespoons water in a microwave-safe dish and stir to combine. Cover with a lid or plastic wrap and cook for 2 minutes on high until tender. Alternatively, place the apple, cinnamon, sugar and ¼ cup water in a small saucepan. Cover and simmer over low heat for 5 minutes or until the apple is soft.

✳ Pears also work really well with this recipe.

Ruby red rhubarb

1 bunch rhubarb, trimmed and cut into 4 cm pieces
2 tablespoons brown sugar
½ teaspoon mixed spice

Place all the ingredients in a medium saucepan over low heat and stir until the sugar dissolves. Increase the heat and simmer for 10 minutes or until the rhubarb is tender. Set aside to cool.

Everyday fruit salad

1 orange, peeled and cut into pieces
1 red apple, cut into small pieces
1 banana, sliced
1 pear, cut into pieces
½ punnet strawberries, each berry hulled and cut in half
16 green grapes, cut in half
pulp of 2 passionfruit

Place all the ingredients in a bowl and gently mix together.

Summery fruit salad

1 mango, peeled and stone removed, cut into thick slices
1 peach, stone removed, cut into thin wedges
250 g pineapple, peeled and cut into 3 cm pieces
2 kiwi fruit, peeled and cut into thin wedges
1 × 425 g can lychees, drained

Place all the ingredients in a bowl and gently mix together.

Pink fruit salad

2 pink grapefruit, peeled and segmented
1 red papaya, peeled, seeded and cut into wedges
300 g watermelon, cut into 2 cm pieces
1 punnet strawberries, each berry hulled and cut in half
½ punnet raspberries (optional)

Place all the ingredients in a bowl and gently mix together.

✱ You could replace the pink grapefruit and papaya
   with 3 medium red apples and 3 medium plums.

lunchbox
foods

Curried chicken and celery

Avocado, grated carrot and cheese

sandwich fillings

Make sure lunches survive the journey to lunchtime by including an ice pack or bottle of frozen water (which will thaw during the day) in the lunchbox. All recipes here make 2 sandwiches. For convenience, make up larger batches of these sandwich fillings and store in the fridge to use over a few days.

Curried chicken and celery

Place 100 g barbecued chicken (or leftover roast chicken) in a bowl with 2 tablespoons fat-reduced natural yoghurt, ½ teaspoon curry powder, 1 stick celery, finely diced, 2 teaspoons mango chutney and 1 tablespoon chopped coriander (optional). Lightly spread 4 slices of wholemeal bread with margarine. Place baby spinach on 2 slices of bread, top both slices with the chicken mixture and sandwich with the remaining bread slices. Cut into fingers.

Chicken, avocado and corn

Mash half an avocado with 2 teaspoons lemon juice. Spread the avocado over 2 slices of wholemeal flatbread (such as Mountain Bread or Lebanese). Divide 100 g shredded chicken, ½ cup shredded lettuce and 125 g can corn kernels, drained, between the 2 flatbreads. Roll up firmly.

Avocado, grated carrot and cheese

Spread 4 wholegrain sandwich crackers with 2 tablespoon light cream cheese. Top 2 crackers with thin slices of avocado and ½ cup grated carrot. Sprinkle with 1 tablespoon sultanas and top with the remaining crackers. If not eating immediately, sprinkle with a few drops of lemon juice to stop the avocado and carrot from browning.

Mashed egg and lettuce

Peel 2 hard-boiled eggs, place in a bowl and roughly mash with a fork. Add 2 teaspoons fat-reduced mayonnaise and ½ teaspoon curry powder and mix until well combined. Lightly spread 2 wholegrain rolls with margarine. Place 2 shredded lettuce leaves in each roll and top with the egg mixture.

Tuna, tomato, grated carrot and lettuce

Lightly spread 4 slices of multigrain bread with margarine. Place 50 g tuna in spring water, drained, in a bowl and stir in 1 tablespoon fat-reduced mayonnaise, 2 roma tomatoes, cut into 1 cm dice, and ½ cup grated carrot. Place a lettuce leaf on each spread side of bread and spread the tuna mixture over 2 slices. Sandwich with the remaining bread slices and cut in half.

Roast beef, chutney and tomato

Cut 2 wholemeal pita breads in half. Split the halves open and spread each half with 2 teaspoons chutney. Divide 1 cup rocket, 2 tomatoes, sliced, and 100 g roast beef, shredded, among the bread halves.

Salmon, lettuce and cucumber

Cut 2 wholemeal bagels in half and spread with 1 tablespoon fat-reduced mayonnaise mixed with 1 tablespoon chopped dill (optional). Place 2 lettuce leaves on the bottom of each bagel, followed by 50 g smoked salmon (or canned salmon, drained) per bagel and some finely sliced cucumber. Put the bagel tops on.

Tomato, cheese and pesto

Spread 2 tablespoons pesto over 2 pieces of wholemeal Lebanese flatbread. Divide ½ cup grated fat-reduced cheddar, 8 cherry tomatoes, quartered, and ¼ cup salad sprouts between the 2 pieces of bread. Roll up firmly.

Corn and pea fritters

Serves 4

¾ cup wholemeal self-raising flour
½ cup fat-reduced milk
2 eggs
½ red capsicum, seeded and finely diced
1½ cups frozen pea and corn mix
1 small red onion, finely diced
olive oil spray

Combine all the ingredients, except the olive oil spray, in a large bowl. Heat a frying pan over medium heat and lightly spray with olive oil. Working in batches, add ¼ cup scoops of mixture to the pan and cook for 4 minutes each side until cooked through and golden. This recipe should make 8 fritters.

✱ Drop tablespoons of mixture into the pan to make bite-sized fritters for a party. These fritters can be frozen and used for snacks.

Banana pikelets

Makes 25

¾ cup wholemeal self-raising flour
1 tablespoon brown sugar
1 cup fat-reduced milk
1 egg
1 ripe banana, mashed
½ teaspoon ground cinnamon
canola oil spray

Sift the flour into a large mixing bowl. Stir in the sugar and make a well in the centre. Whisk together the milk, egg, banana and cinnamon in a jug. Pour into the well and mix until combined. Set aside for 10 minutes to rest.

Heat a frying pan over medium heat and lightly spray with canola oil. Drop tablespoons of batter into the pan and cook for 1 minute until bubbles appear. Turn over and cook for another minute until lightly golden and cooked through. Serve warm or cold.

✱ The pikelets can be frozen and used for snacks.

Egg and ham pies

Makes 6

6 slices wholemeal bread, crusts removed
margarine
100 g lean ham, chopped
3 eggs
½ cup fat-reduced natural yoghurt
1 tablespoon finely chopped chives or other
    fresh herb (optional)

Preheat the oven to 200°C. Lightly spread each slice of bread with margarine and push, spread-side down, into six ⅓ cup muffin holes.

Sprinkle half the ham into the bread cups. Whisk together the eggs, yoghurt and chives with a fork, and spoon into the bread cups. Sprinkle with the remaining ham and bake for 20 minutes until the bread is golden and the egg has set.

✱ These pies can be eaten cold as a lunchbox alternative to sandwiches.

✱ Large batches of these pies can be stored in the freezer for up to a month.

Variations

Baked bean pies

Fill the bread cups from the basic recipe with a mixture of 200 g salt-reduced baked beans and 3 lightly beaten eggs. Sprinkle over the 6 bread cups 3 tablespoons grated fat-reduced cheddar. Bake as in the basic recipe.

Tuna and egg pies

Fill the bread cups from the basic recipe with a mixture of 200 g canned tuna in spring water, drained, 125 g canned corn, drained, and 3 lightly beaten eggs. Bake as in the basic recipe.

Spinach and feta pies

Heat 2 tablespoons olive oil in a small frying pan over medium heat. Add 2 handfuls of baby spinach leaves. Cook for 30 seconds or until wilted. Mix 50 g fat-reduced feta, crumbled, and 3 lightly beaten eggs. Fold in the spinach then spoon into the bread cups. Bake as in the basic recipe.

Egg and ham pies

Cheesy vegie muffins

Cheesy vegie muffins

Makes 12

olive oil spray
2 cups self-raising flour
   (half wholemeal flour, half white flour)
1½ cups fat-reduced milk
2 eggs, lightly beaten
100 g margarine, melted
2 zucchini, coarsely grated
2 carrots, coarsely grated
½ cup grated fat-reduced cheddar
½ teaspoon dried mixed herbs
¼ cup grated fat-reduced cheddar, extra,
   for sprinkling

Preheat the oven to 200°C. Spray 12 × ⅓ cup muffin holes with olive oil.

Sift the flour into a large mixing bowl. Place the milk, egg and margarine in a small jug and whisk lightly with a fork. Pour onto the flour and stir to combine. Fold in the zucchini, carrot, cheddar and mixed herbs. Spoon into the prepared tin and sprinkle with the extra cheese. Bake for 20 minutes, or until the muffins spring back when lightly touched. Cool on a wire rack before serving.

✱ These muffins are ideal to freeze, and perfect for the lunchbox.

Variations

Tuna and corn muffins

Replace the vegies in the basic mixture with 200 g canned tuna in spring water, drained, and 125 g canned corn, drained. Bake as in the basic recipe.

Pea and ham muffins

Replace the vegies, cheese and herbs in the basic recipe with a mixture of 100 g sliced lean ham, roughly chopped, 100 g frozen peas, 1 tablespoon chopped flat-leaf parsley (optional) and 100 g fat-reduced feta (or cheddar), crumbled. Bake as in the basic recipe.

Capsicum and zucchini muffins

Replace the vegies and cheddar in the basic recipe with a mixture of 100 g roasted or fresh red capsicum, chopped, 2 zucchini, coarsely grated, and 100 g grated fat-reduced mozzarella. Bake as in the basic recipe.

Avocado and corn dip

Carrot and chickpea dip

Red capsicum and lentil dip

dips with yummy dippers

Minted pea and cucumber yoghurt dip

Beetroot dip

White bean and tuna dip

Minted pea and cucumber yoghurt dip

1 cup fat-reduced natural yoghurt
1 teaspoon ground cumin (optional)
1 cucumber, seeded and coarsely grated
¾ cup frozen minted peas,
    thawed and roughly mashed
2 teaspoons lemon juice
1 teaspoon mint sauce

Place all the ingredients in a bowl
and stir to combine.

Carrot and chickpea dip

2 medium carrots, coarsely grated
400 g can chickpeas, drained and rinsed
1 clove garlic, crushed
1 tablespoon tahini
¼ cup orange juice
2 tablespoons olive oil

Place all the ingredients in a blender and whiz
until smooth.

✳ Tahini is sesame paste, most commonly
    recognised for its use in making hummus.
    You will often find it in the Middle Eastern
    section of the supermarket. If there is a seed
    allergy in the family, replace the tahini with
    another tablespoon of olive oil.

Beetroot dip

450 g can baby beets, drained
½ cup fat-reduced cottage cheese
    or natural yoghurt
1 teaspoon garam masala
2 tablespoons orange juice
1 tablespoon lemon juice

Place all the ingredients in a blender and whiz
until smooth.

✳ Garam masala is an Indian spice blend,
    available in the spices section of the
    supermarket. It is generally made up
    of ground cumin, coriander, cinnamon,
    nutmeg, cloves and cardamom.

Avocado and corn dip

2 ripe avocados, peeled and mashed
½ small red onion, finely chopped
310 g can creamed corn
2 tablespoons lemon juice
1 teaspoon ground cumin
1 tablespoon roughly chopped coriander
    (optional)
1 red capsicum, finely diced

Place all the ingredients in a bowl
and stir to combine.

Red capsicum and lentil dip

450 g jar roasted capsicums, drained
½ teaspoon ground cumin
2 teaspoons ground coriander
1 clove garlic, crushed (optional)
400 g can brown lentils, drained and rinsed
½ cup fat-reduced natural yoghurt

Place all the ingredients in a blender and whiz until smooth.

White bean and tuna dip

200 g can tuna in spring water, drained
400 g can cannellini beans, drained and rinsed
2 tablespoons lemon juice
½ cup fat-reduced natural yoghurt
1 tablespoon capers in brine,
**   drained and chopped (optional)**
2 tablespoons chopped parsley

Place the tuna, cannellini beans, lemon juice and yoghurt in a blender and whiz until smooth. Transfer to a bowl and stir in the capers and parsley.

Dippers

Serve the dips with a range of dippers:

Carrot and celery soldiers
Baby cucumber boats, seeds scooped out
**   and filled with dip**
Steamed broccoli and cauliflower florets
Oven-baked pita chips
Steamed pumpkin and sweet potato fingers
Wholemeal or wholegrain bread sticks
Capsicum swords
Wholemeal, wholegrain or rye crackers

main meals

Cheese and tomato jaffle

almost instant

Here are some ideas for simple light dinners you can pull together in an instant using basic ingredients – perfect for those nights when everyone is hungry or the cook is low on energy! To make each dish more filling, the savoury recipes can be served with a side salad, some baked beans or a mug of vegie soup.

Cheese and tomato jaffle
Serves 2

4 slices wholemeal or multigrain bread
margarine
1 tablespoon fruit chutney
6 thin slices tomato
2 slices (40 g) fat-reduced cheddar

Preheat a sandwich maker. Lightly spread the bread with margarine. Place 2 slices of bread in the sandwich maker, spread-side down. Spread each slice of bread with chutney, then top with the tomato slices and cheddar. Place the remaining bread slices on top, spread-side up, and toast until golden. Cool slightly, then cut in half and serve.

Variations
Banana and sultana jaffle
Replace the filling in the basic recipe with 1 ripe banana, mashed, and 2 tablespoons sultanas. Toast as in the basic recipe.

Egg and ham jaffle
Replace the filling in the basic recipe with 2 boiled eggs, mashed, topped with 25 g lean shaved ham. Toast as in the basic recipe.

Baked bean and cheese jaffle
Replace the filling in the basic recipe with 130 g salt-reduced baked beans and 2 slices (40 g) fat-reduced cheddar. Toast as in the basic recipe.

Tuna, corn and mayo jaffle

Replace the filling in the basic recipe with a mixture of 90 g canned tuna in spring water, drained, 130 g canned corn, drained, 1 tablespoon fat-reduced mayonnaise and 2 tablespoons shredded basil. Toast as in the basic recipe.

Tuna, mayo and spring onion jaffle

Replace the filling in the basic recipe with a mixture of 90 g canned tuna in spring water, drained, 1 tablespoon fat-reduced mayonnaise and 2 spring onions, finely sliced. Toast as in the basic recipe.

Roast chicken, cheese and spring onion jaffle

Replace the filling in the basic recipe with a mixture of 100 g leftover roast chicken, 2 slices (40 g) fat-reduced cheddar and 2 spring onions, finely sliced. Toast as in the basic recipe.

✳ Precooked, cooled jaffles are great as lunchbox foods and are a way to get more vegetables into your child's diet. Just avoid the messier fillings, such as baked beans.

Ham and cheese omelette
Makes 1

2 eggs
1 tablespoon fat-reduced milk
canola oil spray
2 tablespoons grated fat-reduced cheddar
20 g lean ham, roughly chopped
1 tomato, chopped
wholegrain toast, to serve
garden salad (page 213), to serve

Crack the eggs into a bowl. Add the milk and whisk with a fork until well combined. Spray a medium frying pan with canola oil and place over medium–high heat until foaming. Quickly pour in the egg mixture, tilting the pan to cover the base.

Sprinkle the omelette with the cheese and ham. Cook for 1–2 minutes or until the base is set and golden, and the cheese is beginning to melt. Use a spatula or fork to fold the edge of the omelette towards the centre, then fold in the other side. Tilt the pan away from you and flip the omelette onto a plate. Sprinkle with chopped tomato and serve with wholegrain toast and a garden salad.

Variations
Mushroom and cheese omelette
Replace the ham in the basic recipe with pre-cooked mushroom. Finely slice 4 or 5 button mushrooms. Spray a pan with canola oil and cook the mushrooms for 4 minutes until they begin to brown. Remove from the pan and continue with the basic recipe, replacing the ham with the mushroom.

Leftover roast vegie omelette
Replace the ham and tomato in the basic recipe with ⅓ cup chopped leftover chargrilled vegetables (see recipe on page 212).

✱ Omelettes are a good way to use up leftover cooked meats and vegetables.

✱ If you have herbs growing in a pot or in your garden, use a few finely chopped sprigs in the omelette. Herbs that work well include basil, thyme, chervil and oregano.

Green eggs and ham
Serves 2

1 tablespoon margarine
4 eggs, at room temperature
¼ cup fat-reduced milk
2 tablespoons finely chopped parsley
50 g lean sliced ham
2 × 9-grain English muffins, halved and toasted
garden salad (see page 213), to serve

Melt half the margarine in a medium frying pan over medium heat until sizzling.

Whisk together the eggs, milk and parsley. Pour into the hot pan and, using a spatula or wooden spoon, push the cooked egg towards the centre of pan until all the egg is just set. Remove the pan from the heat.

Spread the muffins with the remaining margarine. Divide the ham among the muffins and top with the green eggs. Serve with a garden salad.

Boiled egg with Vegemite soldiers
Serves 1

2 teaspoons white vinegar
1 egg
1 slice wholemeal toast, spread with margarine and Vegemite, cut into fingers

Bring a medium saucepan of water to the boil and add the vinegar (this will stop the egg from leaking out of the shell if there is a crack). Gently lower the egg into the boiling water and cook for 4½ minutes.

Place the egg in an egg cup and serve with the Vegemite soldiers.

Egg in a hole
Serves 1

1 teaspoon margarine
1 thick slice wholemeal bread
1 egg

Lightly spread both sides of the bread with margarine. Using a 5 cm round cutter, cut out the centre of the bread. Heat a frying pan over medium heat. Place the bread in the pan and cook for 1 minute until golden. Turn the bread over and crack the egg into the 'hole'. Cook for 2 minutes or until the egg has set to your liking.

✱ Serve this or the recipe above with a mug of salt-reduced vegetable soup for lunch or a light dinner.

Boiled egg with Vegemite soldiers

Basic vegetable stir-fry

Basic vegetable stir-fry
Serves 4

2 tablespoons canola oil

1 red onion, cut into wedges

2 cloves garlic, crushed

1 tablespoon finely grated ginger (optional)

handful of green beans, trimmed and
    cut into 2 cm pieces

1 red capsicum, cut into strips

medium head broccoli, cut into florets

handful of snow peas, trimmed

10 mushrooms, sliced

2 tablespoons oyster or soy sauce

¼ cup coriander leaves (optional)

2 cups cooked brown or white rice
    (made from ⅔ cup uncooked rice),
    to serve

Heat a wok over high heat. Add the oil and heat until just smoking, then add the onion, garlic and ginger and stir-fry for 1 minute until the onion starts to soften.

Add the beans, capsicum, broccoli, snow peas and mushrooms and cook for 2 minutes until the mushrooms are soft and the beans are bright green.

Stir in the oyster sauce and 2 tablespoons water and cook for a further minute. Sprinkle with coriander, if using, and serve with rice.

✳ When cooking a stir-fry, start by putting the rice on to boil and cook according to the packet instructions. By the time the rice is cooked, the stir-fry will be ready.

✳ The key to a successful stir-fry is preparing all the ingredients before you start cooking, so that everything cooks together quickly.

✳ You could replace the oyster sauce with soy sauce, if you like.

Variations
Beef and vegetable stir-fry
After following the first step in the basic recipe, add to the onion mixture 500 g lean beef strips and cook for 2 minutes or until golden brown. Add 2 carrots, finely sliced, 1 red capsicum, cut into strips, and 150 g snow peas, trimmed. Cook for 2 minutes until the snow peas are bright green. Continue with the basic recipe.

Prawn, broccoli and green bean stir-fry

After following the first step in the basic recipe, add to the onion mixture 500 g peeled uncooked prawns and cook for 2 minutes or until golden. Add a handful of green beans, cut into 2 cm slices, 1 red capsicum, cut into strips, and a medium head of broccoli, cut into florets. Cook for 2 minutes until the beans are bright green. Continue with the basic recipe.

Chicken, mushroom and corn stir-fry

After following the first step in the basic recipe, add to the onion mixture 500 g chicken strips and cook for 2 minutes or until golden brown. Add a handful of green beans, cut into 2 cm slices, 1 red capsicum, cut into strips, 150 g baby corn, halved lengthways, and 10 button mushrooms, each mushroom halved. Cook for 2 minutes until the mushrooms are tender. Continue with the basic recipe.

* If you like, add 1 tablespoon sweet chilli sauce along with the oyster sauce in this and the recipe above.

Lamb, pumpkin and broccoli stir-fry

Before starting the stir-fry, peel half a butternut pumpkin and cut into 2 cm cubes. Place in a microwave-safe dish, add ¼ cup water, then cover and cook on high for 2 minutes until softened. Proceed with the first step of the basic recipe. Add to the onion mixture 500 g lean lamb strips and cook for 2 minutes or until golden brown. Add a large handful of sugar snap peas, a medium head of broccoli, cut into florets, and the pre-cooked pumpkin. Continue with the basic recipe.

* Beef strips could be used instead of lamb in this recipe.

Sticky sesame tofu and mixed pea stir-fry

After following the first step in the basic recipe, add to the onion mixture a large handful of snow peas, trimmed, a large handful of sugar snap peas, 1 cup frozen peas and 1 red capsicum, cut into strips. Cook for 2 minutes until the peas are bright green. Add 600 g firm tofu, cut into bite-sized cubes, and cook for 2 minutes until heated through. Add 1 tablespoon honey, 1 tablespoon oyster sauce and 1 tablespoon sesame seeds and cook for another minute. Serve sprinkled with coriander leaves, if using, and rice, as per the basic recipe.

Prawn, broccoli and green bean stir-fry

Zucchini, pumpkin and chickpea couscous

Zucchini, pumpkin and chickpea couscous
Serves 4

400 g butternut pumpkin,
    peeled and cut into 4 cm cubes

2 tablespoons olive oil

1 cup couscous

2 zucchini, finely sliced

grated zest and juice of 1 lemon

400 g can chickpeas, drained and rinsed

1 cup salt-reduced vegetable stock

¼ cup roughly chopped coriander (optional)

¼ cup roughly chopped mint (optional)

½ cup fat-reduced natural yoghurt, to serve

Preheat the oven to 200°C. Place the pumpkin in a roasting tin and drizzle with 1 tablespoon olive oil. Roast for 20 minutes until golden and tender. Note, for a quick dinner, pre-roast the pumpkin the day before or use leftover roasted vegetables.

Place the couscous, zucchini, lemon zest, lemon juice and chickpeas in a heatproof bowl and stir to combine. Bring the stock to the boil in a small saucepan over high heat. Pour on the stock and remaining oil, cover tightly with plastic wrap and set aside for 5 minutes until the couscous has absorbed the liquid and the zucchini is tender.

Fluff the couscous with a fork to separate the grains. Stir in the herbs and pumpkin. Divide among four serving dishes and serve with a dollop of yoghurt.

✱ Leftover roast meat or chargrilled vegetables are ideal for use in a couscous dish.

✱ You can use vegetable or chicken stock for couscous.

Variations

Chickpea, sweet potato and spinach couscous
Replace the pumpkin in the basic recipe with 300 g sweet potato, peeled and cut into 3 cm cubes. Proceed with the recipe, omitting the zucchini. Once the couscous has absorbed the liquid, stir in the roast sweet potato, 2 tablespoons blanched almonds (leave out if nut allergy in family) and 75 g baby spinach leaves.

Salmon, tomato and pea couscous
Replace the vegetables in the basic recipe with 1 cup frozen peas and 2 tomatoes, diced. Proceed with the recipe. Once the couscous has absorbed the liquid, stir in 400 g canned salmon, drained and flaked.

Lamb, tabouleh and white bean salad

salads for lunch or dinner

These salads are substantial meals in their own right, ideal for lunch or dinner. You could substitute leftover roast meat for the meat used in several of these dishes.

Lamb, tabouleh and white bean salad
Serves 4

1 cup burghul
2 cups boiling water
1 tablespoon olive oil
500 g lamb back straps
1 teaspoon ground cumin
400 g can cannellini beans, drained and rinsed
1 cup roughly chopped flat-leaf parsley
2 vine-ripened tomatoes, cut into 2 cm dice
2 tablespoons lemon juice
½ cup fat-reduced natural yoghurt
1 tablespoon mint sauce

Place the burghul a heatproof bowl, pour on the boiling water and set aside for 20 minutes to soften.

Heat the oil a large frying pan over medium heat. Sprinkle both sides of the lamb with the cumin and cook for 4 minutes each side. Remove from the pan and place on a plate. Cover loosely with foil and rest for 5 minutes.

Strain the burghul though a fine mesh sieve, pressing with the back of a spoon to remove excess water. Return to the bowl. Add the beans, parsley, tomatoes and lemon juice and stir to combine.

In a small bowl, mix together the yoghurt and mint sauce.

Cut the lamb into 2 cm thick slices and serve with the tabouleh and white bean salad, and a dollop of minted yoghurt.

✱ Burghul is sometimes called 'bulgur'. It is coarsely cracked wheat and is available in supermarkets.

Moroccan lamb and carrot salad
Serves 4

2 carrots, thinly sliced

1 red onion, cut into thin wedges

2 tablespoons Moroccan seasoning

500 g lamb fillet, cut into 3 cm slices

1 tablespoon olive oil

½ cup fat-reduced natural yoghurt

2 tablespoons roughly chopped coriander

1 Lebanese (short) cucumber, coarsely grated

2 tablespoons pine nuts, lightly toasted

100 g baby spinach leaves

1 punnet cherry tomatoes, each tomato halved

wholemeal pita bread, to serve

Combine the carrot, onion, Moroccan seasoning, lamb and olive oil in a large bowl. Set aside for 10 minutes so the flavours develop.

Heat the oil in a large frying pan over medium heat, add the lamb mixture and cook for 8–10 minutes until the lamb is golden and cooked to your liking. Transfer to a large bowl and set aside to cool slightly.

Spoon the yoghurt into a small bowl, add the coriander and cucumber and mix well.

Add the pine nuts, spinach and tomatoes to the lamb and toss to combine. Serve with the cucumber yoghurt and pita bread.

✽ A 400 g can of drained and rinsed brown lentils or chickpeas may be added to the dish.

Moroccan lamb and carrot salad

Vietnamese pork and cabbage salad

Vietnamese pork and cabbage salad
Serves 4

500 g pork fillet, thinly sliced
1 tablespoon canola oil
¼ Chinese cabbage, finely shredded
1 cup bean sprouts, trimmed
1 red capsicum, seeded and finely sliced
1 carrot, coarsely grated
4 spring onions, finely sliced on an angle
¼ cup mint leaves, torn
¼ cup roughly chopped coriander
¼ cup roasted peanuts,
    roughly chopped (optional)

Dressing
¼ cup lime juice
2 teaspoons fish sauce
1 tablespoon sweet chilli sauce
1 teaspoon sesame oil

To make the dressing, place all the ingredients in a screw-top jar and shake well to combine.

Combine the pork and canola oil in a large bowl. Heat a large frying pan over high heat, add the pork and cook until golden and cooked through. Set aside to cool.

Place the cabbage, bean sprouts, capsicum, carrot, spring onion and herbs in a large bowl. Add the pork and dressing and toss to combine. Divide the salad among serving bowls and serve sprinkled with peanuts.

✳ Omit the nuts if there is a nut allergy in the family.

Beef, tomato and sweet potato salad
Serves 4

300 g sweet potato,
    peeled and cut into 1 cm slices
2 tablespoons olive oil
500 g rump steak, fat trimmed
¼ cup pesto
2 tablespoons fat-reduced mayonnaise
12 baby roma tomatoes, halved lengthways
400 g can cannellini beans, drained and rinsed
1 Lebanese (short) cucumber,
    cut into 2 cm dice
1 green butter lettuce, leaves separated

Preheat the oven to 200°C and line a baking tray with baking paper.

Place the sweet potato slices on the baking tray and drizzle with 1 tablespoon oil. Bake for 15 minutes or until tender and golden.

Heat a large frying pan over medium–high heat. Brush the steak with the remaining oil and cook for 4 minutes each side for medium, or until cooked to your liking. Place on a plate and cover loosely with foil. Rest for 5 minutes, then cut into 1 cm thick slices.

Combine the pesto and mayonnaise in a small bowl, adding 2 teaspoons of warm water if the mixture is too thick.

Place the tomatoes, beans, cucumber, lettuce, sweet potato and beef slices in a large bowl. Drizzle with half the pesto mayonnaise and toss to combine. Divide among serving plates, drizzle with the remaining mayonnaise and serve.

Ploughman's plate
Serves 4

80 g fat-reduced cheddar, cut into 4 pieces
1/3 cup fruit chutney
2 cups green salad leaves
2 red apples, cored and cut into quarters
2 sticks celery, cut in half
2 carrots, cut into 6 cm sticks
8 baby beets, halved
400 g rare roast beef slices
4 small wholemeal grain rolls
   or 4 slices wholemeal bread

Honey mustard dressing
1 tablespoon honey
1 tablespoon seeded mustard
1/4 cup fat-reduced mayonnaise

To make the dressing, place all the ingredients in a screw-top jar, add 2 tablespoons warm water and shake well to combine.

Divide the ploughman's ingredients among four plates, drizzle the salad leaves with the dressing and serve. Alternatively, set out each ingredient on its own small serving dish and let everyone help themselves.

Caesar salad boats
Serves 4

4 slices wholemeal bread, cut into 1 cm dice
olive oil spray
6 rashes lean rindless bacon, finely chopped
4 baby cos lettuces, leaves separated
2 Lebanese (short) cucumber,
   cut into 1 cm dice
1 punnet cherry tomatoes, each tomato halved
1/3 cup finely grated parmesan
3/4 cup fat-free Caesar dressing

Preheat the oven to 200°C and line a baking tray with baking paper. Place the bread dice and bacon on the baking tray, spray with olive oil and bake for 10 minutes until golden and the bacon is crisp. Set aside to cool.

Choose eight cos lettuce cups of a similar size and set aside. Finely shred the remaining lettuce and combine in a bowl with the cucumber, tomatoes, parmesan and dressing.

Fill the lettuce cups with the salad, top with the croutons and bacon and serve immediately.

✳ Add leftover roast chicken to these Caesar salad boats to make a more substantial meal.

Ploughman's plate

Caesar salad boats

Niçoise salad
Serves 4

12 chat potatoes, halved
large handful of green beans, trimmed
4–6 eggs
1 cos lettuce, washed and cut into 5 cm slices
4 roma tomatoes, cut into wedges
400 g canned tuna in spring water, drained
½ cup pitted Kalamata olives

Dressing
¼ cup extra virgin olive oil
¼ cup white wine vinegar
1 teaspoon seeded mustard

Place the potatoes in a saucepan of cold water, bring to the boil over high heat and cook for 8 minutes or until just tender. Add the beans and cook for a further minute. Drain and refresh under cold running water.

Bring a small saucepan of water to the boil over high heat, add the eggs and cook for 6 minutes. Drain and cool under cold running water. Peel the eggs and cut into quarters.

To make the dressing, place all the ingredients in a screw-top jar and shake well to combine.

Divide the cos among serving bowls or arrange on a large platter. Top with the potatoes, beans, eggs, tomatoes, tuna and olives. Drizzle the dressing over the top and serve.

✱ If you don't have cos lettuce to hand, by all means use iceberg lettuce.

Niçoise salad

Salmon and pea quiche

patties and savoury bakes

These recipes are great for casual dinners and light meals. Many of them can be used as leftovers for lunch or a snack the next day. Or put extra portions away in the freezer for a rainy day.

Salmon and pea quiches
Serves 4 for a light meal or 2 for dinner

canola oil spray
4 sheets filo pastry
4 eggs
150 g fat-reduced natural yoghurt
grated zest and juice of ½ lemon
½ cup frozen peas, thawed
210 g canned red salmon, drained and flaked
1 tablespoon finely sliced chives (optional)
1 tablespoon finely chopped mint (optional)
garden salad (see page 213), to serve

Preheat the oven to 180°C. Spray four ½ cup muffin holes with canola oil.

Lightly spray one sheet of filo with canola oil and fold it in half. Spray the filo again and fold it in half; spray and fold one more time, then press into a muffin hole. Repeat with the remaining sheets of filo to make four cases.

Lightly whisk the eggs and yoghurt in a bowl. Stir in the lemon zest and juice, peas, salmon, chives and mint (if using). Spoon into the filo cases and bake for 20 minutes until set. Serve with a garden salad.

✱ You can make a batch of these little quiches to freeze. They will keep, well wrapped, in the freezer for a month. Reheat straight from the freezer in a preheated 180°C oven for 15 minutes or until warmed through.

Mushroom, spinach and feta mini frittatas
Serves 4

1 tablespoon olive oil
200 g button mushrooms, sliced
1 small head broccoli, cut into florets
1 red onion, finely sliced
150 g baby spinach leaves
8 eggs
400 g fat-reduced natural yoghurt
100 g fat-reduced feta, crumbled
garden salad (see page 213), to serve

Preheat the oven to 180°C. Line 8 × ⅓ cup muffin holes with paper cases.

Heat the oil in a frying pan over medium heat and cook the mushrooms, broccoli and onion for 3 minutes until soft. Add the spinach and continue cooking until the spinach is just wilted.

Place the eggs, yoghurt and feta in a bowl and whisk together lightly. Stir in the mushrooms, broccoli, onion and spinach. Spoon the mixture into the paper cases and bake for 10 minutes or until set. Serve warm or at room temperature with a garden salad.

✱ You could use grated cheddar instead of feta cheese.

✱ This could also be cooked in one large, shallow ovenproof dish.

✱ Slices of frittata make a great addition to lunchboxes.

Corn, capsicum and spinach frittata
Serves 6

800 g waxy potatoes, cut into 3 cm chunks
2 tablespoons olive oil
1 small red onion, finely sliced
195 g can corn, drained
1 capsicum, seeded and cut into 2 cm pieces
100 g button mushrooms, thinly sliced
1 bunch English spinach, leaves washed and roughly chopped
8 eggs, lightly beaten
2 tablespoons chopped parsley

Place the potato in a small saucepan of cold water. Bring to the boil over medium heat and cook for 8 minutes until tender. Drain and leave to cool slightly.

Preheat the griller to hot.

Heat the oil in a large heavy-based frying pan over high heat and cook the onion and potato for 3 minutes until golden. Add the corn, capsicum and mushrooms and cook for 2 minutes until the capsicum begins to soften. Stir in the spinach, egg and parsley and give the pan a gentle shake to even out the mixture. Reduce the heat to medium–low and cook for 8–10 minutes until the base of the frittata is golden and the egg is beginning to set. Place under the griller and cook for a further 5 minutes until golden and set. Cut into slices and serve with warm wholemeal pita bread spread with mashed avocado.

Corn, capsicum and spinach frittata

Baked sweet potatoes with beef, tomato and cheese

Baked sweet potatoes with beef, tomato and cheese
Serves 4

2 × 500 g sweet potatoes
1 tablespoon olive oil
1 small red onion, halved and diced
500 g lean minced beef
½ teaspoon mixed dried herbs
2 tomatoes, diced
1 tablespoon tomato sauce
1 cup frozen mixed vegetables
80 g fat-reduced cheddar, grated
4 small wholegrain bread rolls,
    spread thinly with margarine, to serve
garden salad (see page 213), to serve

Preheat the oven to 180°C. Wrap each sweet potato in foil and roast on the oven rack for 45 minutes or until soft. Remove from the foil and cut in half lengthways. Scoop out the potato flesh, then roughly mash and set aside.

Meanwhile, heat the oil a large frying pan over medium heat and cook the onion for 2 minutes, or until soft. Add the beef and cook for 4–5 minutes until golden. Add the dried herbs, tomatoes and tomato sauce. Reduce the heat and simmer for 10 minutes, or until the tomatoes have collapsed. Add the mixed vegetables and sweet potato mash and cook for 1 minute until heated through.

Line a baking tray with baking paper. Spoon the beef mixture into the potato cases. Place the potatoes on the baking tray and sprinkle with cheese, then cook in the 180°C oven for 15 minutes until the cheese is melted and golden. Serve with the bread rolls and a garden salad.

✱ This recipe also works well with regular potatoes rather than sweet potatoes.

Variations

Baked potatoes with tuna, corn and mixed vegies

Follow the first step of the basic recipe, using regular rather than sweet potatoes. Mix 185 g canned tuna in spring water, drained and flaked, 125 g canned corn, drained, 2 tablespoons finely sliced spring onions, 1 cup frozen mixed vegetables, thawed, ¼ cup fat-reduced natural yoghurt and 2 tablespoons chopped parsley (optional) with the potato mash. Spoon the mixture into the potato cases and bake as in the basic recipe.

Baked potatoes with salmon and leek

Follow the first step of the basic recipe, using regular rather than sweet potatoes. Heat 1 tablespoon olive oil in a frying pan over medium heat and cook 1 finely sliced leek for 3 minutes until soft. Mix together 185 g canned salmon, drained and flaked, 2 tablespoons fat-reduced cream cheese, the leek and the potato mash. Spoon the mixture into the potato cases and bake as in the basic recipe.

Baked sweet potatoes with roast chicken and salsa

Follow the first step of the basic recipe. Mix 500 g chopped roast chicken, ½ cup tomato salsa and the sweet potato mash. Bake as in the basic recipe.

Zucchini and vegetable slice
Serves 4 for lunch

1 cup wholemeal self-raising flour
1 small red onion,
    halved and finely sliced
3 zucchini, coarsely grated
2 carrots, coarsely grated
1 small sweet potato,
    peeled and coarsely grated
¼ cup coarsely grated parmesan
4 eggs
½ cup fat-reduced milk
1 teaspoon dried thyme (optional)
½ cup grated fat-reduced cheddar
garden salad (page 213), to serve

Preheat the oven to 200°C. Line a 20 cm square cake tin with baking paper.

Place the flour, onion, zucchini, carrot, sweet potato and parmesan in a bowl and stir until well combined. Make a well in the centre. Whisk together the eggs, milk and thyme (if using) in a jug, pour into the well and mix until well combined. Spoon into the cake tin, sprinkle with the cheddar and bake for 25 minutes until golden and firm to the touch. Serve with a garden salad.

Yummy beef rissoles
Serves 4

500 g lean minced beef
1 small brown onion, very finely diced
1 tablespoon fruit chutney
1 tablespoon barbecue sauce
1 egg, lightly beaten
2 tablespoons dried wholegrain breadcrumbs
¼ cup finely chopped parsley (optional)
2 tablespoons olive oil
1 tablespoon plain flour
2 cups salt-reduced beef stock
1 tablespoon Worcestershire sauce
golden mash (page 212), to serve
steamed green beans, to serve

Combine the minced beef, onion, chutney, barbecue sauce, egg, breadcrumbs and parsley (if using) in a large bowl. Mix with your hands until well combined, then divide the mixture evenly into 8 portions and shape into patties.

Heat the oil in a large frying pan over medium heat. Add the rissoles in batches and cook for 3 minutes each side until browned and cooked through. Remove from the pan and set aside.

Add the flour to the pan and stir into the pan juices with a wooden spoon. Slowly add the beef stock, stirring constantly to make a smooth gravy, then add the Worcestershire sauce.

Return the rissoles to the pan and cover with a lid or foil. Simmer for 15 minutes until cooked through. Serve with golden mash and green beans.

✱ Rissoles will become crumbly if the onion is too chunky, so be sure to dice it very finely.

Tuna bake
Serves 4

250 g shell pasta
2½ cups salt-reduced chicken stock
½ cup fat-reduced milk
2 tablespoons margarine
2 tablespoons plain flour
2 sticks celery, finely sliced
400 g can tuna in spring water, drained
1 cup frozen pea and corn mix
medium head broccoli, cut into small florets
1 cup grated fat-reduced cheddar
½ cup dried wholemeal breadcrumbs
¼ cup roughly chopped parsley (optional)

Preheat the oven to 200°C. Bring a large saucepan of water to the boil, add the pasta and cook according to the packet instructions. Drain and refresh under cold running water.

Pour the stock and milk into a microwave-safe jug and heat on high power for 40 seconds. Alternatively, place in a small saucepan over low heat for about 5 minutes or until hot.

Melt the margarine in a saucepan over medium heat, add the flour and stir to a smooth paste. Slowly add the stock mixture, stirring constantly to make a smooth sauce. Simmer for 2 minutes, then stir in the celery, tuna, pea and corn mix, broccoli and ½ cup cheddar. Add the pasta, then pour the mixture into a ceramic baking dish. Mix the breadcrumbs, remaining cheese and parsley (if using) and sprinkle over the pasta. Bake for 20 minutes or until the crust is crisp and golden.

Macaroni and vegie bake
Serves 4

300 g macaroni
1½ cups fat-reduced milk
1 cup salt-reduced chicken stock
¾ cup grated fat-reduced cheddar
¼ cup grated parmesan
2 tablespoons margarine
2 tablespoons plain flour
2 roma tomatoes, cut into 2 cm cubes
2 zucchini, coarsely grated
1 cup baby beans, cut into 3 cm pieces

Bring a large saucepan of water to the boil, add the pasta and cook according to the packet instructions. Drain and refresh under cold running water.

Pour the milk and stock into a microwave-safe jug and heat on high power for 40 seconds. Alternatively, place in a small saucepan over low heat for about 5 minutes or until hot. Combine the cheddar and parmesan in a small bowl. Preheat the grill to hot.

Melt the margarine in a saucepan over medium heat, add the flour and stir to a smooth paste. Slowly add the stock mixture, stirring constantly to make a smooth sauce. Stir in half the cheese and simmer for 2 minutes. Add the tomato, zucchini and beans and cook for 2 minutes or until the beans are tender and bright green. Stir through the cooked pasta. Spoon into a shallow ovenproof dish or individual dishes and sprinkle with the remaining cheese. Place under the grill for 3 minutes until the cheese is melted and golden brown.

Macaroni and vegie bake

Potato and lentil cakes
Serves 4

300 g waxy potatoes,
    peeled and cut into 4 cm chunks
2 × 400 g cans brown lentils, drained
    and rinsed
½ small red onion, finely diced
1 clove garlic, crushed
2 teaspoons garam masala (optional)
1 teaspoon curry powder
½ cup roughly chopped coriander
1 egg, lightly beaten
½ cup dried wholemeal breadcrumbs
2 tablespoons olive oil

Place the potato in a small saucepan of cold water. Bring to the boil over medium heat and cook for 8 minutes until tender. Drain and leave to cool slightly.

Combine the potato and lentils in a large bowl and mash until smooth. Stir in the onion, garlic, garam masala, curry powder, coriander and egg. Divide the mixture evenly into 8 portions and shape into patties.

Gently roll the patties in the breadcrumbs, then place in the refrigerator for 20 minutes to firm up.

Heat the oil in a large frying pan over medium heat. Add the patties in batches and cook for 3 minutes each side until golden brown and cooked through.

✱ Garam masala is an Indian spice blend, available in the spices section of the supermarket.

Chicken potato cakes with cucumber yoghurt
Serves 4

200 g waxy potatoes,
    peeled and cut into 4 cm chunks
200 g sweet potatoes,
    peeled and cut into 4 cm chunks
250 g cooked chicken
1 cup frozen mixed vegetables,
    thawed and drained
1 egg, lightly beaten
½ cup dried wholemeal breadcrumbs
2 tablespoons finely chopped parsley
    (optional)
1 tablespoon olive oil
½ Lebanese (short) cucumber
½ cup fat-reduced natural yoghurt

Place the potato and sweet potato in a saucepan of cold water. Bring to the boil over medium–high heat and cook for 8 minutes until tender. Drain and mash, then set aside to cool.

Combine the potato mash, chicken, vegetables, egg, breadcrumbs and parsley (if using) in a large bowl. Mix with your hands, then divide the mixture evenly into 8 portions and shape into patties. Refrigerate for 30 minutes before cooking.

Heat the oil in a large frying pan over medium heat. Add the patties in batches and cook for 4 minutes each side until golden brown and cooked through.

Quarter the cucumber lengthways then finely slice. Stir through the yoghurt. Serve dolloped onto the potato cakes.

Chicken potato cakes

Fettuccine with tomato, tuna and lemon

pasta and basic sauces

Master just a couple of basic pasta sauces and you'll be able to create lots of delicious and varied pasta meals. Try a range of different pasta shapes to keep kids interested.

Fettuccine with tomato, tuna and lemon
Serves 4

250 g fettuccine
2 tablespoons olive oil
400 g can diced tomatoes
3 spring onions or 1 small onion, finely sliced
1 tablespoon capers, roughly chopped (optional)
grated zest and juice of 1 lemon
2 tablespoons torn basil (optional)
185 g can tuna in oil, drained and flaked
¼ cup roughly chopped parsley
garden salad (see page 213), to serve

Bring a large saucepan of water to the boil and cook the fettuccine according to the packet instructions. Drain and set aside.

Heat the oil in a large frying pan over medium heat, then add the tomatoes and onion and simmer for 2 minutes. Stir in the capers, lemon zest and juice, basil, tuna and 2 tablespoons parsley and cook for 5 minutes. Add the fettuccine and toss to combine. Sprinkle the remaining parsley over the top and serve with a garden salad.

Tomato pasta sauce
Serves 4

1 onion, roughly chopped
1 carrot, roughly chopped
2 sticks celery, roughly chopped
¼ cup salt-reduced tomato sauce
1 teaspoon dried oregano
1 teaspoon dried Italian herbs
2 cloves garlic, crushed
2 × 400 g cans chopped tomatoes
1 cup salt-reduced vegetable stock

Place all the ingredients in a large heavy-based saucepan over medium heat. Bring to the boil, then reduce the heat and simmer for 20 minutes. Remove from the heat and set aside to cool slightly. Place the sauce in a food processor or use a hand-held blender to blend until smooth.

Simply serve stirred through cooked pasta (or filled fresh pasta, such as tortellini) and top with parmesan.

✱ Batches of this sauce can be made and stored in the freezer.

Quick uses for tomato pasta sauce
Creamy salmon and tomato fettuccine
Add 400 g canned salmon, drained and flaked, and ½ cup fat-reduced natural yoghurt to the basic sauce. Serve with cooked fettuccine.

Chicken, pea and tomato pasta bows
Add 500 g cooked, shredded chicken and 2 cups frozen peas to the basic sauce. Simmer for 1 minute. Serve with cooked pasta bows.

Polka-dot pumpkin and spinach cannelloni
Serves 4

350 g butternut pumpkin, coarsely grated
250 g frozen chopped spinach,
    thawed and drained
½ cup fat-reduced ricotta
½ cup fat-reduced natural yoghurt
2 tablespoons pesto
4 fresh lasagne sheets, halved widthways,
    or 12 instant dried cannelloni tubes
2 cups tomato pasta sauce (see adjacent
    recipe) or store-bought tomato pasta sauce
8 bocconcini, halved,
    or 1 cup grated fat-reduced cheese

Preheat the oven to 180°C. Mix the pumpkin, spinach, ricotta, yoghurt and pesto in a bowl.

Place the pasta sheets on a clean surface. Spoon ½ cup of the pumpkin mixture across the short side of each lasagne sheet and roll up to form a tube shape (you should have 8 in all). Alternatively, use a teaspoon to tightly fill 12 instant dried cannelloni tubes.

Spread ½ cup tomato sauce over the base of a ceramic baking dish and place the tubes on top. Cover with the remaining sauce and dot the bocconcini over the top. Bake for 30 minutes, if using fresh lasagne sheets, or 45 minutes if using dried cannelloni tubes, or until al dente.

Creamy mushroom sauce
Serves 4

30 g dried shiitake mushrooms (optional)
1 tablespoon olive oil
1 small onion, finely chopped
300 g button mushrooms, finely sliced
¼ cup fat-reduced cream cheese
¼ cup roughly chopped parsley

If you are using the dried mushrooms, place them in a heatproof bowl and cover with 1½ cups boiling water. Set aside for 5 minutes to rehydrate, then strain, reserving the liquid. Finely slice the mushrooms and set aside.

Heat the oil in a frying pan over medium heat and cook the onion for 2 minutes until soft. Add the button and shiitake mushrooms and cook for 3 minutes until golden and soft. Stir in the reserved mushroom liquid (or, if you are not using shiitake mushrooms, add 1 cup salt-reduced vegetable stock or water) and cream cheese and simmer for 5 minutes until the sauce starts to thicken. Stir in the parsley. Serve with any cooked pasta.

Other uses for creamy mushroom sauce

Baked potato with mushroom sauce
Preheat the oven to 180°C. Wrap a large potato in foil and roast on the oven rack for 45 minutes or until soft. Spoon over the mushroom sauce.

Sauce for meats
Serve creamy mushroom sauce over grilled chicken breast, steak or pork chops.

Spaghetti with mushrooms, ham and broccoli
Serves 4

250 g spaghetti
1 head broccoli, cut into florets
1 quantity of creamy mushroom sauce
   (see adjacent recipe)
100 g lean sliced ham
¼ cup grated parmesan

Bring a large saucepan of water to the boil and cook the spaghetti according to the packet instructions. About 2 minutes before the spaghetti is ready, add the broccoli to the pan and cook until tender. Drain and set aside.

Heat the mushroom sauce in a large frying pan over medium heat, add the ham and simmer for 2 minutes. Stir in the spaghetti and broccoli. Divide among 4 serving dishes and sprinkle with parmesan.

Penne with chicken, capsicum and mushrooms
Serves 4

250 g penne
2 tablespoons olive oil
500 g chicken tenderloins, cut into 4 cm pieces
1 red onion, finely sliced
1 red capsicum, seeded and finely sliced
1 yellow capsicum, seeded and finely sliced
1 quantity of creamy mushroom sauce
   (see page 193)

Bring a large saucepan of water to the boil and cook the penne according to the packet instructions. Drain and set aside.

Heat the oil in a large frying pan over medium heat and cook the chicken for 3 minutes until golden. Add the onion and capsicum and cook for 2 minutes until the vegetables are soft. Add the mushroom sauce and simmer for 2 minutes until heated through. Stir in the pasta and serve.

Quick baked fusilli and meatballs
Serves 4

500 g minced pork and veal
2 spring onions or 1 small onion, finely sliced
2 tablespoons dried wholemeal breadcrumbs
1 egg
½ cup roughly chopped parsley
½ cup finely grated parmesan
1 quantity of tomato pasta sauce
   (see page 192) or 1 × store-bought
   750 ml bottle of tomato pasta sauce
250 g fusilli pasta

Preheat the oven to 200°C. Combine the minced pork and veal, onion, breadcrumbs, egg, half the parsley and half the parmesan in a large bowl. Roll into 20 even-sized balls.

Spoon the tomato pasta sauce into a large ceramic baking dish. Stir in the uncooked pasta and place the meatballs on top. Bake for 25 minutes or until the meatballs are cooked through and pasta is tender. Stir in the remaining parsley and serve sprinkled with the remaining parmesan.

Penne with chicken, capsicum and mushrooms

Quick baked fusilli and meatballs

Fried rice

rice

These recipes are great for a simple, casual dinner and can easily be bulked out to feed extra hungry mouths. Leftovers are delicious the next day.

Fried rice
Serves 4

canola oil spray
2 eggs, lightly beaten
1 small onion, finely chopped
1 clove garlic, crushed
3 cm piece ginger, peeled and finely grated
large head broccoli, cut into small florets
1 cup frozen mixed Asian vegetables, thawed and drained
2 cups cooked brown or white rice (made from $^2/_3$ cup uncooked rice)
400 g leftover roast beef, lamb or chicken
2 tablespoons sesame seeds, lightly toasted (optional)
4 spring onions, finely sliced
2 tablespoons roughly chopped coriander (optional)
2 tablespoons oyster sauce or salt-reduced soy sauce

Heat a large frying pan over high heat and spray with canola oil. Add the egg, tilting the pan to cover the base, and cook for 1 minute or until just set. Remove from the pan and roll into a cigar shape. Finely slice and set aside.

Lightly spray the pan again, then add the onion, garlic and ginger and cook for 3 minutes until the onion is soft. Add the broccoli and mixed vegetables and cook for 3 minutes until the broccoli is tender and bright green.

Add the rice and beef, lamb or chicken and cook for a further 2 minutes. Stir in the egg strips, sesame seeds, spring onion, coriander and oyster sauce. Serve immediately.

✱ The key to good fried rice is that the rice be day-old. This is a great way to use up leftover cooked rice from last night's dinner. Freshly cooked rice will be too soggy.

✱ Omit the sesame seeds if there is a seed allergy in the family.

Basic pea and parmesan risotto

Basic pea and parmesan risotto
Serves 4

1 litre salt-reduced chicken stock
2 tablespoons olive oil
1 onion, finely chopped
2 cloves garlic, crushed
1 cup Arborio rice
1½ cups frozen peas
¼ cup finely grated parmesan

Heat the stock in a medium saucepan over high heat. Reduce the heat to low and keep at a gentle simmer.

Heat the oil in a large saucepan over medium heat. Add the onion and garlic and cook, stirring, for 5 minutes or until the onion softens.

Add the rice and stir with a wooden spoon for 1–2 minutes until it is well coated in the oil. Add ½ cup stock and stir constantly until all the liquid has been absorbed. Continue adding the stock, ½ cup at a time, making sure the liquid is completely absorbed before adding more. This should take about 20 minutes; check that the rice is tender.

Add the peas and cook, stirring, for 2 minutes or until heated through. Stir in the grated parmesan, and serve immediately.

✱ Leftover risotto is a handy snack, which can be reheated for afternoon tea.

Variations
Carrot, pumpkin and zucchini risotto
When adding the stock, stir in ½ cup grated carrot, 1 cup grated pumpkin and 2 grated zucchini. Continue with the recipe.

Leftovers risotto
When adding the peas, stir in 350 g leftover roast chicken, beef or lamb or 400 g canned tuna or salmon, drained.

Seafood paella

Serves 4

2 tablespoons olive oil

1 onion, finely chopped

1 clove garlic, crushed

1 teaspoon paprika

½ teaspoon ground turmeric

1 red capsicum, cut into 1 cm dice

1 cup Arborio rice

400 g can chopped tomatoes

3 cups salt-reduced chicken stock

150 g salmon fillet, skin removed, cut into 4 cm cubes

150 g firm white fish fillets, skin removed, cut into 4 cm cubes

200 g seafood marinara mix

150 g frozen pea and corn mix

grated zest and juice of 1 lemon

½ cup roughly chopped flat-leaf parsley (optional)

garden salad (see page 213), to serve

Heat the oil in a large frying pan over medium heat and cook the onion and garlic for 2 minutes or until the onion is soft. Add the paprika, turmeric, capsicum and rice and stir for 2 minutes until the rice is well coated in the spiced oil.

Add the tomatoes and stock and simmer, uncovered, for 10 minutes, stirring occasionally. Place the fish pieces and seafood on the rice, then cover and simmer for a further 10 minutes until the rice is tender.

Stir in the pea and corn mix, lemon zest and juice. Cover and set aside for 5 minutes, then sprinkle with parsley (if using). Serve with a garden salad.

Seafood paella

Mexican vegetable rice

Mexican vegetable rice
Serves 4

1 tablespoon olive oil

1 onion, sliced

1 clove garlic, crushed

1 red capsicum, seeded and finely sliced

2 teaspoons ground cumin

1 teaspoon ground coriander

½ teaspoon mild paprika

1 cup rice

grated zest and juice of 1 lime or lemon

400 g can chopped tomatoes

2 cups salt-reduced vegetable stock

400 g can red kidney beans, drained
and rinsed

1 cup corn kernels

½ cup roughly chopped coriander (optional)

½ cup tomato salsa

Heat the oil in a large saucepan over medium heat and cook the onion and garlic for 2 minutes until the onion softens. Add the capsicum, cumin, coriander, paprika, rice, juice and zest, tomatoes and stock. Bring to the boil, then reduce the heat to low, cover and simmer for 10–12 minutes or until the rice is tender. Stir in the kidney beans and corn. Remove from the heat and set aside for 3 minutes. Sprinkle with coriander and serve with salsa.

✱ This is also great as a side dish for 6 or 8 served with grilled or barbecued meats.

Lemony lamb pilaf
Serves 4

2 tablespoons olive oil

500 g lamb leg steaks, cut into 4 cm cubes

1 onion, finely diced

2 cloves garlic, crushed

1 cup pearl barley

1 teaspoon dried oregano

grated zest and juice of 1 large lemon

3 cups salt-reduced chicken stock

½ head cauliflower, cut into small florets

1½ cups frozen peas

Preheat the oven to 180°C. Heat the oil in a large ovenproof stockpot over medium heat, add the lamb and cook for 1 minute each side until browned. Remove from the pan. Add the onion and garlic and cook for 3 minutes or until soft.

Stir in the barley, oregano and lemon zest and cook for 1 minute, stirring constantly. Add the stock, cauliflower and lemon juice and bring to the boil. Return the lamb to the pan, then cover and bake for 35 minutes or until the barley is tender.

Remove the dish from the oven and stir in the peas. Cover and set aside for 5 minutes before serving.

Chicken noodle salad

roasts and ideas for leftovers

Everyone loves a roast dinner: the aroma of the meat cooking and the communal atmosphere as the family eats together. But equally as good are the many ways you can use the leftovers for delicious meals later in the week.

How to cook roast chicken
Serves 6 (or 4 plus leftovers)

1 × 1.4 kg chicken
1 tablespoon olive oil
1 lemon, halved
2 sprigs rosemary, roughly chopped
2 sprigs lemon thyme, roughly chopped
potatoes, pumpkin or parsnips,
    peeled and cut into 4 cm chunks

Preheat the oven to 220°C. Rinse the chicken under cold running water and pat dry with paper towel. Trim any excess fat from the cavity, then tuck the wings underneath. Place the chicken on a wire rack in a roasting tin, breast-side up.

Combine the olive oil and lemon juice in a small bowl (keep the lemon skins).

Place the rosemary, thyme and lemon skins in the chicken cavity and tie the legs together with kitchen string. Drizzle the lemon oil over the top and roast for 1 hour.

Add the vegetables to the tin and cook for 30 minutes or until the juices of the chicken run clear when the thick part of the thigh is tested with a skewer, and the vegetables are golden.

Remove from the oven. Cover the chicken loosely with foil. Set aside to rest for 15 minutes. Serve with the roast vegetables.

Chicken noodle salad
Serves 4

100 vermicelli (glass) noodles
500 g roast chicken, shredded
1 large yellow capsicum, finely sliced
1 large red capsicum, finely sliced
1 carrot, finely sliced
1 cup bean sprouts or snow pea shoots
150 g snow peas, trimmed

Dressing
1 tablespoons salt-reduced soy sauce
1 tablespoon olive oil
juice of 1 lime or lemon
1 tablespoon grated fresh ginger

Place the vermicelli noodles in a large heatproof bowl. Cover with boiling water and set aside for 5–10 minutes until the noodles are soft. Drain and refresh under cold running water. Roughly chop and place in a large bowl.

Add the chicken, yellow and red capsicum, carrot, bean sprouts and snow peas. Toss gently.

In a separate bowl, whisk together the soy sauce, olive oil, lime or lemon juice and ginger. Drizzle over the salad and serve.

Chicken and rocket penne
Serves 4

200 g wholemeal penne
1 tablespoon olive oil
1 red onion, finely sliced
1 large red capsicum, finely sliced
1 large or 2 small zucchini, sliced
500 g roast chicken, shredded
1 cup tomato pasta sauce (see page 192)
or store-bought tomato pasta sauce
2 tablespoons grated parmesan
150 g baby rocket or spinach leaves

Bring a large saucepan of water to the boil and cook the penne according to the packet instructions. Drain and set aside.

Meanwhile, heat the olive oil in a large frying pan over medium heat. Add the onion, capsicum and zucchini and cook for 2 minutes or until the vegetables start to soften. Add the chicken and pasta sauce and cook for 2 minutes, stirring, until the sauce is smooth.

Stir in the parmesan and baby rocket or spinach. Serve with the cooked penne.

Chicken tortillas
Serves 4

⅓ cup fat-reduced hummus
4 wholemeal tortillas
2 cups shredded lettuce
2 tomatoes, diced
¼ cup grated carrot
¼ cup grated zucchini
500 g roast chicken, shredded
⅓ cup Mexican tomato salsa

Spread the hummus over the tortillas. Divide the lettuce, tomato, carrot, zucchini and chicken among the tortillas. Top with the tomato salsa and roll up.

✱ You might like to serve the fillings in separate bowls at the table so that everyone can assemble their own tortilla.

How to cook roast lamb
Serves 6 (or 4 plus leftovers)

2.4 kg leg of lamb
1 tablespoon finely chopped rosemary
finely grated zest and juice of 1 lemon
2 cloves garlic, crushed
2 teaspoons Dijon mustard
potatoes, pumpkin or parsnips,
    peeled and cut into 4 cm chunks
frozen peas, cooked according to packet
    instructions, to serve

Preheat the oven to 200°C. Trim the visible fat from the leg of lamb and score diagonally at 1 cm intervals.

Combine the rosemary, lemon zest and juice, garlic and mustard in a small bowl and rub all over the lamb. Place the lamb on a rack in a roasting tin and pour 1 cup water into the base. Cover with foil and roast for 30 minutes, then remove the foil and roast for a further 30 minutes.

Add the vegetables to the roasting tin. Continue to cook for a further 30 minutes.

Remove from the oven and cover the lamb loosely with foil. Set aside to rest for 15 minutes. Carve into thin slices (about three slices per person) and serve with the roast vegetables and peas.

Roast lamb, currant and beetroot salad
Serves 4

500 g roast lamb, sliced
2 Lebanese (short) cucumbers,
    finely sliced on an angle
1 small red onion, finely sliced
2 tablespoons currants
3 cups green leaves (such as rocket,
    butter lettuce, baby spinach,
    cos or mixed leaves)
12 canned baby beets, drained and halved

Dressing
2 tablespoons mint sauce
¼ cup roughly chopped coriander (optional)
¼ cup fat-reduced natural yoghurt

Place the roast lamb slices in a large bowl. Add the cucumber, onion, currants and green leaves. Toss gently to combine. Top with the baby beets.

In a separate small bowl mix together the mint sauce, coriander, if using, and yoghurt. Drizzle over the salad.

Lamb and barley hotpots

Lamb and barley hotpots
Serves 4

1 tablespoon oil
1 onion, finely sliced
2 tablespoons wholemeal flour
½ cup pearl barley
1 litre salt-reduced chicken stock
grated zest and juice of 1 lemon
500 g roast lamb, roughly chopped
3 sticks celery, sliced
2 carrots, sliced
large handful green beans, chopped
2 tablespoons chopped parsley

Heat the oil in a large saucepan over medium heat and cook the onion for 3 minutes until soft. Add the flour and barley, and stir to combine. Gradually add the chicken stock and lemon zest and juice, stirring constantly. Add the lamb, celery and carrot. Bring to the boil, then reduce the heat and simmer for 20 minutes until the barley is tender.

Place the green beans in a microwave-safe dish. Add ¼ cup water, then cover and cook on high for 2 minutes.

Stir in the green beans and parsley, and serve.

Lamb risoni
Serves 4

1 tablespoon oil
1 onion, finely diced
1 clove garlic, crushed
2 teaspoons garam masala
400 g can chopped tomatoes
3 cups salt-reduced beef stock
2 teaspoons finely grated lemon zest
¾ cup risoni
500 g roast lamb, roughly chopped
1 cup frozen peas
150 g baby spinach leaves

Heat the oil in a large frying pan over medium heat. Add the onion, garlic and garam masala, and cook for 2 minutes until the onion is soft. Add the canned tomatoes, beef stock, lemon zest and risoni. Bring to the boil, then reduce the heat and simmer for 10 minutes until the risoni is tender.

Stir in the lamb, peas and spinach leaves. Simmer until warmed through and serve.

✳ Garam masala is an Indian spice blend, available in the spices section of the supermarket.

✳ Risoni looks like rice but is in fact a pasta, and can be found in the pasta section of the supermarket. It's ideal for use in salads and soups.

Golden mash

Ratatouille

Bubble and squeak
patties

Vegie slaw

easy vegetable sides

Rainbow chips

Traditional roast vegies

Chargrilled vegetables

Golden mash
Serves 4

300 g parsnips, peeled and chopped
300 g sweet potatoes, peeled and diced
300 g pumpkin, peeled and diced
¼ cup fat-reduced milk

Place the vegetables in a large saucepan, cover with cold water and bring to the boil over high heat. Reduce the heat and simmer for 15 minutes or until tender. Drain and return to the saucepan. Add the milk and mash until smooth (or blend in a food processor if preferred).

Rainbow chips
Serves 4

2 parsnips, peeled and cut into 6 cm chips
2 medium potatoes, cut into 6 cm chips
3 carrots, cut into 6 cm chips
1 sweet potato, peeled and cut into 6 cm chips
1 beetroot, peeled and cut into thin wedges
2 zucchini, cut into quarters lengthways and halved
1 teaspoon dried rosemary
1 teaspoon garlic powder
2 tablespoons olive oil

Preheat the oven to 200°C and line two baking trays with baking paper. Place all the vegetables on the baking trays and sprinkle with rosemary and garlic powder. Drizzle with the olive oil and bake for 35 minutes until golden, swapping the trays around halfway through the cooking time.

Chargrilled vegetables
Serves 4

1 red capsicum, thickly sliced
1 bunch asparagus, trimmed and halved
2 zucchini, cut into 1 cm slices on an angle
6 yellow squash, halved
1 eggplant, cut into 1 cm rounds
olive oil spray
1 tablespoon olive oil
2 teaspoons balsamic vinegar

Heat a chargrill pan or barbecue to high. Lightly spray the vegetables with olive oil, then add to the pan in batches and cook for 3 minutes each side until soft. Transfer to a bowl or serving dish, drizzle with olive oil and balsamic vinegar and serve.

Traditional roast vegetables
Serves 4

500 g butternut pumpkin, peeled and cut into 4 cm chunks
250 g potato, peeled and cut into 2 cm slices
2 parsnips, peeled and cut into 4 cm chunks
2 tablespoons olive oil
1 teaspoon dried mixed herbs

Preheat the oven to 200°C. Place the vegetables in a large baking dish, then drizzle with the oil and sprinkle with the mixed herbs. Roast the vegetables for 20 minutes, then turn them over and cook for a further 20 minutes until tender and golden.

Bubble and squeak patties
Serves 4

300 g pumpkin, peeled and cut into chunks
2 medium potatoes, quartered
300 g sweet potato, peeled and cut into chunks
½ cup frozen pea and corn mix
¼ cup grated fat-reduced cheese

Preheat the oven to 200°C and line a baking tray with baking paper. Place the chopped vegetables in a medium saucepan, cover with cold water and bring to the boil over medium heat. Reduce the heat and simmer for 15 minutes or until tender. Stir in the pea and corn mix, then drain and roughly mash. Set aside to cool slightly, then stir in the cheese. Shape into patties and bake in the oven for 10 minutes until golden.

Vegie slaw
Serves 4

2 small zucchini, coarsely grated
2 small carrots, coarsely grated
1 red onion, finely sliced
½ baby Chinese cabbage, finely shredded
1 red capsicum, finely sliced
½ cup fat-reduced mayonnaise
grated zest and juice of 1 lemon
1 tablespoon sesame seeds, lightly toasted

Combine the zucchini, carrot, onion, cabbage and capsicum in a large bowl. In a separate bowl, whisk together the mayonnaise and lemon juice. Pour the dressing over the vegetables and mix well. Sprinkle with sesame seeds, then serve.

Ratatouille
Serves 4

1 tablespoon olive oil
1 red onion, finely chopped
1 clove garlic, finely chopped
1 medium eggplant, cut into 2 cm chunks
1 red capsicum cut into 2 cm chunks
4 yellow squash, quartered
2 green zucchini, cut into 1 cm slices
400 g can chopped tomatoes
1 teaspoon mixed dried herbs

Heat the oil in a large saucepan over medium heat and cook the onion and garlic for 2 minutes until soft. Add the eggplant and capsicum and cook for 5 minutes until the eggplant starts to soften. Add the squash, zucchini, chopped tomatoes and herbs. Bring to the boil, then reduce the heat and simmer, covered, for 15 minutes, stirring occasionally.

Garden salad
Serves 4

½ iceberg lettuce, roughly chopped
1 avocado, peeled and diced
½ punnet cherry tomatoes, each tomato halved
1 Lebanese (short) cucumber, halved lengthways and thickly sliced
1 red capsicum, cut into thin strips
¼ cup store-bought French dressing

Place the lettuce, avocado, tomatoes, cucumber and capsicum in a large serving bowl. Drizzle over the dressing. Toss gently to combine.

Beef and vegetable noodles

weekday dinners

This is when every minute counts. Try these quick, no-fuss recipes for nutritious weekday dinners that will keep everyone in the family satisfied.

How to cook the perfect steak

Heat a frying pan over medium heat. Lightly brush 4 pieces scotch fillet, rump, sirloin or fillet steak with light olive oil, rather than oiling the pan. Cook the steak for 3–4 minutes each side for medium (based on a 2.5 cm thickness). Turn the steak once only using tongs. Transfer the steak to a plate, cover loosely with foil and rest for 5 minutes (this will result in a more tender steak). Serve with salad or steamed vegetables.

✱ The same method may be used for barbecuing – preheat the barbecue to medium high (180°C if you have a thermostat).

Beef and vegetable noodles
Serves 4

500 g sirloin steak, trimmed of fat
1 tablespoon olive oil
2 cm piece ginger, peeled and grated
150 g mushrooms, sliced
1 red onion, halved and cut into
    thin wedges
large handful of sugar snap peas
1 head broccoli, cut into small florets
1 red capsicum, finely sliced
2 tablespoons oyster sauce
2 cups fresh egg noodles

Heat a frying pan over medium heat. Lightly brush the steak with olive oil, add to the pan and cook for 3–4 minutes each side for medium, or until cooked to your liking. Transfer the steak to a plate, cover loosely with foil and rest for 5 minutes. Cut into thin slices.

While the meat is resting, heat the remaining oil in the frying pan and cook the ginger, mushrooms and onion for 3 minutes or until the mushrooms start to soften. Add the sugar snap peas, broccoli, and capsicum and 2 tablespoons water. Cook for 2 minutes or until the sugar snap peas and broccoli are tender and bright green.

Add the oyster sauce, beef and noodles and stir until combined and heated through. Serve immediately.

Veal schnitzel
Serves 4

1½ cups dried multigrain breadcrumbs
1 teaspoon garlic powder
1 teaspoon dried oregano
2 eggs, lightly beaten
4 pieces veal schnitzel (thinly cut veal steaks)
    approximately 125 g each
½ cup plain flour
olive oil spray
handful of green beans,
    trimmed and lightly steamed, to serve
traditional roast vegetables
    (see page 212), to serve

Preheat the oven to 200°C and line a baking tray with baking paper. Mix the breadcrumbs, garlic powder and oregano in a shallow bowl. Pour the beaten egg into another shallow bowl.

Combine the veal schnitzels with the flour in a large snaplock bag and toss to coat. Shake off any excess flour, then dip the veal into the eggs and then into the breadcrumbs. Press the crumbs on firmly.

Place the schnitzels on the baking tray and spray with olive oil. Bake for 10 minutes each side. Serve with steamed green beans and roast vegetables.

✱ Instead of veal, chicken breasts sliced into 2 thin fillets will also work for this recipe.

Sweet and sour pork
Serves 4

2 tablespoons salt-reduced soy sauce
2 tablespoons tomato sauce
1 tablespoon malt vinegar
2 teaspoons brown sugar
2 tablespoons canola oil
500 g pork fillet, cut into 1 cm slices
1 small red onion, halved and cut into thin wedges
1 red capsicum, cut into thin strips
handful of green beans, cut into 2 cm pieces
150 g pineapple pieces
2 bunches bok choy, halved
2 carrots, cut into matchsticks
2 cups cooked brown or white rice (made from
    ⅔ cup uncooked rice)

Combine the soy sauce, tomato sauce, vinegar and brown sugar in a small bowl. Set aside.

Heat 1 tablespoon oil in a large frying pan over medium heat. Add the pork in 2 batches and cook for 2 minutes until golden brown. Set aside on a plate.

Heat the remaining oil in the pan and cook the onion and capsicum for 2 minutes, or until soft. Return the pork to the pan with the beans, pineapple and soy mixture and cook for 2 minutes until the sauce is sticky and heated through.

Place the bok choy and carrot in a microwave-safe dish. Add ¼ cup water, then cover and cook on high for 2 minutes. Alternatively, steam these vegetables over a small saucepan of simmering water and cook for 2 minutes until tender.

Serve with the rice, bok choy and carrot sticks.

How to pan-fry fish

Heat a frying pan over medium heat. Brush 4 × 125 g skinless snapper or bream fillets with a little olive oil and cook for about 3 minutes each side or until the fish flakes when tested with a fork (the exact cooking time will depend on the thickness of the fish). Serve with salad or steamed vegetables.

Baked fish with tomato, onion and lentils
Serves 4

2 zucchini, cut into thin slices

1 red onion, finely sliced

2 tomatoes, diced

2 teaspoons capers, roughly chopped
    (optional)

400 g can brown lentils, drained and rinsed

1 tablespoon olive oil

2 tablespoons lemon juice

4 × 120 g white fish fillets, skin removed
    (try snapper, bream or ling)

2 tablespoons chopped parsley

golden mash (see page 212),
    or garden salad (see page 213), to serve

Mix the zucchini, onion, tomato, capers, lentils, olive oil and lemon juice in a bowl.

Preheat the oven to 190°C.

Place 4 × 30 cm × 30 cm pieces of foil on a flat surface, then top each with a piece of baking paper the same size. Place a quarter of the lentil mixture in the middle of each square of baking paper and place a fish fillet on top. Fold over two sides of the foil and paper, and seal, to make 4 parcels. Place on a baking tray and bake for 15 minutes or until the fish is cooked through. Serve with golden mash or a garden salad.

Honey-soy salmon fingers with baby corn
Serves 4

8 small bamboo skewers (optional)
1 tablespoon sesame seeds
2 tablespoons sweet chilli sauce
1 tablespoon honey
2 tablespoons salt-reduced soy sauce
500 g salmon fillets, skin removed,
    cut into finger-length strips
1 tablespoon canola oil
150 g baby corn, halved lengthways
2 carrots, finely sliced
2 bunches baby bok choy, sliced lengthways
2 cups cooked rice
    (made from ⅔ cup uncooked rice)

If using, soak bamboo skewers for 15 minutes to prevent scorching during the cooking process.

Place the sesame seeds, sweet chilli sauce, honey and 1 tablespoon soy sauce in a bowl. Add the salmon and turn to coat in the marinade, then place in the refrigerator for 10 minutes. Thread the salmon pieces onto the skewers (if using).

Heat 2 teaspoons oil in a large frying pan over medium heat. Add the salmon fingers (in batches if necessary) and cook for 3 minutes. Turn once and cook on the other side for a further 3 minutes, or to your liking. Set aside.

Heat the remaining oil in the pan and cook the baby corn, carrot and bok choy for 4 minutes or until the corn is tender. Drizzle with the remaining soy sauce. Serve the salmon skewers with the vegetables and rice.

Yummy fish burger
Serves 4

500 g white fish fillets, skin removed
2 tablespoons roughly chopped parsley
1 tablespoon finely grated lemon zest
1 tablespoon dried chives (optional)
1 egg
¼ cup dry multigrain breadcrumbs
1 tablespoon olive oil
4 wholemeal bread rolls, halved and toasted
4 lettuce leaves
2 tomatoes, sliced
1 Lebanese (short) cucumber, finely sliced
¼ cup fat-reduced mayonnaise
vegie slaw (see page 213), to serve

Place the fish, parsley, lemon zest, chives and egg in a food processor and whiz until just combined. Transfer to a bowl and add the breadcrumbs. Mix with clean hands, then divide the mixture into 4 balls. Refrigerate for 20 minutes, then gently flatten the balls into patties.

Heat the oil in a large frying pan over medium heat and cook the patties for 4 minutes each side, or until cooked through. On the base of each bread roll place a lettuce leaf and slices of tomato and cucumber on top, followed by a fish patty. Finish with a dollop of mayonnaise. Sandwich with the top half of the roll and serve with vegie slaw.

Yummy fish burger

Lamb kofta with lemon yoghurt

Lamb kofta with lemon yoghurt
Serves 4

12 bamboo skewers (optional)
1 tablespoon olive oil
1 brown onion, very finely chopped
1 clove garlic, crushed
1 teaspoon curry powder
1 teaspoon garam masala (optional)
500 g lean minced lamb
2 tablespoons roughly chopped coriander
1 tablespoon roughly chopped mint (optional)
2 tablespoons lemon juice
canola oil spray
2 cups cooked brown or white rice (made from $^2/_3$ cup uncooked rice)
vegie slaw (see page 213), to serve

Lemon yoghurt
½ cup fat-reduced natural yoghurt
2 tablespoons lemon juice
1 tablespoon roughly chopped coriander

If using bamboo skewers for a 'hand-held' dinner, soak them for 15 minutes to prevent them from scorching during the cooking process.

Heat the oil in a medium frying pan over medium heat and cook the onion and garlic for 3 minutes until the onion is soft. Stir in the curry powder and garam masala, then remove from the heat and set aside to cool.

Combine the onion mixture, minced lamb, coriander, mint and lemon juice in a large bowl. Mix well, then divide evenly into 16 portions and mould into short sausage shapes. If using bamboo skewers, thread each kofta onto a skewer. Cover with plastic wrap and refrigerate for 10 minutes.

To make the lemon yoghurt, combine all the ingredients in a small bowl.

Place a frying pan over high heat. Spray the kofta with canola oil, add to the hot pan and cook for 5 minutes each side until browned and cooked through.

Serve with the lemon yoghurt, rice and vegie slaw.

Sesame chicken drumsticks

How to cook chicken breasts

Heat a frying pan over medium heat, or heat a chargrill to medium–high. Lightly brush 4 small chicken breasts with olive oil, rather than oiling the pan. Cook the chicken for 5 minutes each side, or until cooked through. Transfer to a plate, cover loosely with foil and rest for 5 minutes. Serve with salad or steamed vegetables.

Sesame chicken drumsticks
Serves 4

8 skinless chicken drumsticks (about 700 g)
1 tablespoon sesame seeds
½ cup plum sauce
1 tablespoon honey
1 tablespoon soy sauce
1 red onion, cut into thin wedges
1 red capsicum, cut into 2 cm strips
150 g dried egg noodles
4 cups frozen Asian vegetables, thawed
1 tablespoon plum sauce, extra

Place the chicken, sesame seeds, plum sauce, honey and soy sauce in a large bowl and mix to combine. Cover and refrigerate for 30 minutes.

Preheat the oven to 200°C and line a large baking dish with baking paper. Transfer the chicken to the baking dish and bake for 20 minutes. Turn the chicken pieces over, add the onion and capsicum and bake for a further 25 minutes until the chicken is golden and cooked through.

Bring a saucepan of water to the boil, add the noodles and cook until tender. Add the vegetables and cook for a further 30 seconds. Drain, then stir in the extra plum sauce. Serve the vegetable noodles with the chicken drumsticks.

Tandoori chicken skewers
Serves 4

8 bamboo skewers
500 g skinless chicken thigh fillets, trimmed of fat, cut into 4 cm pieces
2 tablespoons tandoori paste
200 g fat-reduced natural yoghurt
16 cherry tomatoes
2 zucchini, halved lengthways and cut into 2 cm pieces
2 cups cooked brown or white rice (made from ⅔ cup uncooked rice)
2 tablespoons mango chutney

Soak the bamboo skewers for 15 minutes to prevent them from scorching while cooking.

Preheat the oven to 200°C and line a baking tray with baking paper. Place the chicken pieces, tandoori paste and yoghurt in a large bowl and mix until the chicken is well coated. Cover and set aside for 10 minutes.

Thread a piece of chicken, a cherry tomato and a piece of zucchini onto a skewer. Repeat, then continue with the remaining skewers. Place the skewers on the baking tray and cook in the oven for 10–12 minutes or until the chicken is cooked through. Serve with the rice and mango chutney.

Beef and noodle soup

soups for lunch or dinner

These hearty soups are satisfying enough to serve for main meals. Some can be prepared ahead of time to serve on busy nights; others can be made in large batches and frozen.

Beef and noodle soup
Serves 4

100 g dried flat rice noodles
1.5 litres salt-reduced chicken stock
3 cm piece ginger, peeled and
    cut into matchsticks
1 brown onion, finely diced
2 carrots, finely sliced
4 baby bok choy, sliced lengthways
1 red capsicum, sliced
150 g baby corn, halved lengthways
1 tablespoon salt-reduced soy sauce
1 tablespoon oyster sauce
500 g beef rump, trimmed of fat, finely sliced

Place the noodles in a heatproof bowl, cover with boiling water and set aside for 3 minutes until the noodles are soft. Drain and refresh under cold water.

Combine the stock, ginger, onion and carrot in a large saucepan over medium heat. Bring to the boil, then reduce the heat and simmer for 6 minutes or until the carrot is tender. Add the bok choy, capsicum, baby corn, soy and oyster sauce and stir until well combined and warmed through. Add the beef and simmer for a further 2 minutes, until cooked through.

Place the noodles into 4 serving bowls. Ladle the hot soup over the top and serve.

Lamb and vegetable soup
Serves 4

1 tablespoon olive oil
500 g lamb leg steaks, cut into 2 cm cubes
1 small onion, chopped
1 clove garlic, finely chopped
1 teaspoon dried rosemary
2 carrots, sliced
2 sticks celery, sliced
1 litre salt-reduced beef stock
400 g can pureed tomatoes
400 g can chickpeas, drained and rinsed
½ cup frozen peas
½ cup chopped parsley

Heat the oil in a large heavy-based saucepan over medium heat and cook the lamb for 5 minutes until browned. Remove and set aside. Add the onion, garlic, rosemary, carrot and celery to the pan and cook for 3 minutes until soft.

Return the lamb to the pan and add the stock and pureed tomatoes. Bring to the boil, then reduce the heat and simmer for 20 minutes or until the lamb is tender.

Stir in the chickpeas and frozen peas and cook for 1 minute until heated through. Ladle the soup into bowls and sprinkle with the parsley before serving.

Corn and chicken soup
Serves 4

1 tablespoon canola oil

1 brown onion, finely diced

1 stick celery, finely diced

1 clove garlic, crushed

2 cups frozen or canned corn

310 g creamed corn

500 g chicken breast, sliced

1 litre salt-reduced chicken stock

150 g snow peas, trimmed and
   cut into 2 cm pieces

2 tablespoons salt-reduced soy sauce
   (optional)

Heat the oil in a large saucepan over medium heat and cook the onion, celery and garlic for 3 minutes or until soft.

Add the corn kernels, creamed corn, chicken and stock. Bring to the boil, then reduce the heat and simmer for 10 minutes until the chicken is cooked through. Stir in the snow peas and soy sauce (if using), then ladle into bowls and serve.

Pumpkin, carrot and parsnip soup with baby meatballs
Serves 4

1 tablespoon olive oil

1 onion, finely sliced

1 clove garlic, finely chopped

1 teaspoon garam masala (optional)

½ large butternut pumpkin, peeled and diced

3 carrots, sliced

2 parsnips, peeled and sliced

1 litre salt-reduced vegetable stock

½ cup fat-reduced natural yoghurt

Baby meatballs

500 g lean minced veal, beef or lamb

1 teaspoon ground cumin or oregano

1 tablespoon olive oil

Heat the oil in a large heavy-based saucepan over medium heat and cook the onion, garlic and garam masala for 2–3 minutes until soft. Add the pumpkin, carrot and parsnip and stir to coat. Pour in the stock and bring to the boil, then reduce the heat and simmer, covered, for 15 minutes until the vegetables are tender.

Transfer the soup to a blender and whiz until smooth. If necessary, thin it with a little water.

Meanwhile, to make the meatballs, combine the mince and cumin in a bowl. Roll tablespoons of the mixture into balls. Heat the oil in a large frying pan over medium heat, add the meatballs in batches and cook for 5 minutes or until brown and cooked through.

Ladle the soup into bowls and top with yoghurt. Serve with the meatballs.

Pumpkin, carrot and parsnip soup with baby meatballs

Spiced red lentil soup with cheesy subs

Spiced red lentil soup with cheesy subs
Serves 4

1 tablespoon olive oil
2 carrots, finely chopped
1 onion, finely chopped
2 sticks celery, finely chopped
1 clove garlic, crushed
1 cup dried red lentils
1 teaspoon ground cumin
1 teaspoon ground coriander
½ teaspoon ground turmeric
400 g can diced tomatoes
1 litre salt-reduced vegetable stock
2 zucchini, finely chopped
large handful of green beans,
    trimmed and cut into 1 cm pieces

Cheesy subs
4 small wholemeal torpedo bread rolls
80 g grated fat-reduced cheddar

Heat the oil in a heavy-based saucepan over medium heat and cook the carrot, onion and celery for 3 minutes or until the onion is soft. Add the garlic, lentils, cumin, coriander, turmeric, tomatoes and stock. Bring to the boil, then reduce the heat and simmer for 30 minutes or until the lentils are soft. Stir in the zucchini and beans and cook for a further minute.

Meanwhile, to make the cheesy subs, preheat the grill to hot. Cut the rolls in half lengthways and lightly toast. Sprinkle the cheese over the cut side of each roll and grill for 3 minutes until the cheese is melted and golden. Serve the cheesy subs with the soup.

Cauli soup with fish fingers
Serves 4

1 tablespoon olive oil
2 leeks, washed and finely sliced
2 sticks celery, chopped
1 clove garlic, crushed
1 teaspoon dried thyme
1 small–medium cauliflower, cut into florets
1 litre salt-reduced chicken or vegetable stock
½ cup fat-reduced natural yoghurt

Fish fingers
100 g wholemeal plain flour
2 eggs, beaten
1 cup fresh wholemeal breadcrumbs
500 g firm white fish fillets,
    cut into 3 cm thick fingers
olive oil spray

Preheat the oven to 200°C and line a baking tray with baking paper.

Heat the oil in a large saucepan over medium heat and cook the leek, celery, garlic and thyme for 5 minutes. Add the cauliflower and stock. Bring to the boil, then reduce the heat and simmer for 20 minutes until the cauliflower is tender.

Meanwhile, to make the fish fingers, place the flour, egg and breadcrumbs in 3 separate bowls. Dredge the fish in the flour, then in the egg, and finally in the breadcrumbs. Place on the baking tray and lightly spray with olive oil. Bake for 8 minutes or until golden and crisp.

Transfer the soup to a blender, add the yoghurt and whiz until smooth. Ladle into bowls and serve with the fish fingers.

Easy lasagne

slower meals to cook and keep

The following recipes are ideal to cook on the weekend when you have a little more time. That way you will have a delicious home-cooked meal during the week that simply needs reheating.

Easy lasagne
Serves 4

1 quantity of bolognese sauce (see page 232)
4 fresh lasagne sheets or 12 dried instant lasagne sheets
200 g fat-reduced ricotta
½ cup fat-reduced milk
½ cup pizza cheese
garden salad (see page 213), to serve

Preheat the oven to 190°C. Spoon a quarter of the bolognese sauce over the base of a 1.5 litre ceramic baking dish. Place a fresh lasagne sheet over the sauce, trimming with a small knife to fit. Repeat with the remaining sauce and lasagne, finishing with a lasagne sheet. Alternatively, if using dried instant lasagne sheets, use 3 sheets per layer and continue as in the instructions above.

In a small bowl, mix together the ricotta, the milk and half the pizza cheese. Spoon the mixture over the lasagne, smoothing the surface with the back of a spoon. Sprinkle with the remaining cheese and bake for 35 minutes until the pasta is tender and the topping is golden brown. Serve with a garden salad.

✳ This recipe is great to freeze.

✳ Pizza cheese is a mixture of mozzarella, cheddar and parmesan. It is available in most supermarkets, but if you can't find it use grated fat-reduced mozzarella or cheddar instead.

Spaghetti bolognese
Serves 4

1 tablespoon olive oil
1 large brown onion, finely chopped
2 cloves garlic, crushed
1 carrot, finely diced
100 g button mushrooms, sliced
2 sticks celery, finely diced
500 g lean minced beef
1 teaspoon dried mixed herbs
700 ml tomato pasta sauce (see page 192)
   or store-bought tomato pasta sauce
1 zucchini, coarsely grated
150 g pumpkin, coarsely grated
250 g spaghetti (white or wholemeal)
garden salad (see page 213), to serve

Heat the oil in a large frying pan over medium heat and cook the onion for 3 minutes or until soft. Add the garlic, carrot, mushrooms and celery and cook for 2 minutes or until the mushrooms are soft.

Add the mince and cook for 5 minutes until browned, stirring to break up any lumps. Add the mixed herbs, tomato pasta sauce, zucchini and pumpkin. Bring to the boil, then reduce the heat and simmer for 45 minutes.

Cook the pasta according to the packet instructions. Drain and divide among 4 serving bowls. Spoon the bolognese sauce over the top and serve and with a garden salad.

✻ Cook multiple batches of bolognese sauce and freeze for later use. The sauce will keep well in the freezer for 3 months.

Chilli con carne
Serves 4

1 quantity of bolognese sauce
   (see adjacent recipe)
400 g can red kidney beans,
   drained and rinsed
2 teaspoons ground cumin
2 teaspoons ground coriander
2 teaspoons sweet paprika
½ cup salt-reduced beef stock
200 g fat-reduced natural yoghurt
½ avocado, cut into 1 cm cubes
coriander leaves, to garnish (optional)

Place the bolognese sauce, beans, spices and stock in a large saucepan over medium heat. Bring to the boil, then reduce the heat and simmer for 5 minutes until heated through.

Divide among 4 serving bowls and top with a dollop of yoghurt and a scattering of avocado and coriander leaves. Serve with steamed new potatoes and green beans

✻ This recipe is great to freeze.

Variation
Nachos
Preheat the oven to 200°C and line a baking tray with baking paper. Separate the pockets of 2 wholemeal pita breads, then cut each into eight wedges and place on the baking tray. Spray lightly with olive oil spray and bake for 5–10 minutes until golden brown and crisp. Serve with chilli con carne to make nachos.

Country lamb casserole
Serves 4

2 tablespoons wholemeal plain flour

500 g lamb leg steaks, cut into 5 cm cubes

3 tablespoons olive oil

2 small brown onions, cut into 2 cm cubes

2 sticks celery, cut into 1 cm slices

2 carrots, cut into 1 cm cubes

100 g button mushrooms, sliced

1 clove garlic, crushed

2 teaspoons mixed dried herbs

400 g can diced tomatoes

2 teaspoons cornflour

2 cups salt-reduced beef stock

2 parsnips, peeled, halved and cut
   into 3 cm chunks

½ cup frozen peas

2 cups cooked brown or white rice
   (made from ⅔ cup uncooked rice)

Place the flour and lamb in a bag and shake to coat the lamb. Heat 1 tablespoon oil in a large saucepan or casserole dish, add half the lamb and cook for 3 minutes each side or until brown. Transfer to a plate. Heat another tablespoon of oil and cook the remaining lamb. Add to the plate.

Heat the remaining tablespoon of oil in the pan and cook the onion, celery and carrot for 3 minutes or until the onion is soft. Return the lamb to the pan and add the mushrooms, garlic, dried herbs and tomatoes.

Place the cornflour in a jug and gradually add the stock, stirring to prevent any lumps. Add the stock mixture and parsnips to the pan. Bring to the boil, then reduce the heat and simmer for 1 hour until the lamb is tender, stirring occasionally. Stir in the peas until warmed through. Serve with the rice.

Crunchy fish pie
Serves 4

1 teaspoon olive oil
1 teaspoon margarine
1 brown onion, finely diced
1 tablespoon wholemeal plain flour
1 cup fat-reduced milk, warmed
1 cup salt-reduced chicken stock, warmed
500 g salmon fillets, skin removed,
    cut into 3 cm cubes
2 cups frozen pea and corn mix
4 sheets filo pastry
olive oil spray
150 g green beans, trimmed
2 large carrots, cut into matchsticks

Preheat the oven to 180°C. Heat the oil and margarine in a saucepan over medium heat and cook the onion for 2 minutes or until soft. Sprinkle the flour over the onion and stir to combine. Gradually add the milk and stock, stirring constantly to prevent any lumps. Stir in the salmon, peas and corn and simmer for 2 minutes, then spoon the mixture into a 1.5-litre ceramic ovenproof dish.

Cut each sheet of filo in half and lightly spray with olive oil. Scrunch each piece and arrange over the salmon mixture to cover. Bake for 15 minutes until the pastry is golden and crisp.

Place the green beans and carrot in a microwave-safe dish. Add ¼ cup water, then cover and cook on high for 2 minutes. Serve with the fish pie.

Shepherd's pie with a golden top
Serves 4

1 tablespoon olive oil
1 brown onion, finely chopped
2 cloves garlic, crushed
1 carrot, cut into 1 cm cubes
1 stick celery, cut into 1 cm slices
500 g minced lamb
1 teaspoon dried rosemary
400 g can diced tomatoes
2 tablespoons barbecue sauce
1 cup frozen mixed vegetables
1 quantity of golden mash (see page 212)
½ cup grated fat-reduced cheddar

Heat the oil in a large frying pan over medium heat and cook the onion for 3 minutes or until soft. Add the garlic, carrot and celery and cook for 2 minutes or until the carrot starts to soften. Add the mince and cook for 5 minutes, stirring constantly, until browned. Stir in the rosemary, tomatoes, barbecue sauce and ¼ cup water. Bring to the boil, then reduce the heat and simmer for 30 minutes. Stir in the mixed vegetables and remove from the heat.

Preheat the oven to 200°C.

Spoon the mince mixture into 4 × 500 ml ovenproof dishes or a 2-litre baking dish. Top with the golden mash, smoothing the surface with the back of a spoon. Sprinkle with the grated cheese and bake for 20 minutes until golden.

✸ Replace the minced lamb with minced beef to make cottage pie.

Shepherd's pie with a golden top

Yellow pork and vegetable curry

Yellow pork and vegetable curry
Serves 4

2 teaspoons canola oil

500 g pork fillet, cut into 1 cm slices

1 tablespoon yellow curry paste

1 small red onion, halved and cut into thin wedges

2 teaspoons cornflour

1 cup light coconut milk

200 g green beans, trimmed and halved

1 red capsicum, halved, seeded and thinly sliced

200 g snow peas, trimmed and halved

2 cups cooked brown or white rice
   (made from $^2/_3$ cup uncooked rice)

coriander leaves and cucumber slices,
   to garnish (optional)

Heat the oil in a wok or large frying pan over medium–high heat until smoking, then add the pork and cook for 1–2 minutes or until golden. Add the curry paste and onion and stir-fry for 2 minutes or until the onion is soft.

Mix the cornflour, coconut milk and ⅓ cup water until smooth and add to the pan. Bring to the boil and cook for 3 minutes or until thickened slightly. Add the beans, capsicum and snow peas and cook for 2 minutes until the snow peas are bright green and the pork is cooked through.

Divide the rice and curry among serving bowls. Garnish with coriander leaves and cucumber slices, if desired.

✳ As an alternative to light coconut milk try coconut-flavoured evaporated milk, which is also available in supermarkets.

Cheeseburger with beetroot relish

alternatives to takeaways

These recipes are quick to make and fun to eat. When the kids are asking for hamburgers or you feel like fish and chips on a Friday night, consider cooking one of these healthy recipes and you'll save money too.

Cheeseburger with beetroot relish
Serves 4

500 g lean minced beef

1 egg, lightly beaten

½ cup fresh wholemeal breadcrumbs

1 carrot, coarsely grated

1 zucchini, coarsely grated

125 g can corn, drained

1 onion, finely chopped

¼ cup finely chopped parsley

1 tablespoon olive oil

4 slices fat-reduced cheddar

1 cup shredded lettuce or
    baby spinach leaves

2 tomatoes, thickly sliced

4 multigrain bread rolls, lightly toasted

Beetroot relish

225 g can sliced beetroot,
    drained and cut into matchsticks

2 tablespoons brown sugar

2 tablespoons malt vinegar

To make the beetroot relish, place the beetroot, sugar and vinegar in a small saucepan over medium heat and cook for 5 minutes until sticky, stirring constantly. Remove from the heat and set aside to cool.

Combine the mince, egg, breadcrumbs, carrot, zucchini, corn, onion and parsley in a large bowl and mix with your hands until well combined. Roll the mixture into 4 balls, then flatten slightly into patties. Cover and refrigerate for 30 minutes.

Preheat the grill to hot.

Heat the oil in a large frying pan over medium–high heat and cook the patties for 5 minutes each side or until cooked through.

Place the patties on a baking tray, top with a slice of cheese and grill for 3 minutes or until the cheese melts.

Place the lettuce and tomatoes on the base of the rolls, followed by the patties and beetroot relish. Top with the bread lids and serve.

✱ To simplify this recipe, the homemade beetroot relish can be swapped for a store-bought relish or omitted altogether.

Steak sandwich with avocado and tomato relish

Serves 4

4 × 100 g beef minute steaks

8 lettuce leaves

8 slices multigrain bread, lightly toasted

½ avocado, thinly sliced

rainbow chips (see page 212), to serve

Tomato relish

1 tablespoon olive oil

1 small red onion, finely sliced

250 g cherry tomatoes, halved

1 small Granny Smith apple,
    peeled and coarsely grated

2 tablespoons red-wine vinegar

2 tablespoons brown sugar

To make the tomato relish, heat the oil in a small saucepan over medium heat and cook the onion for 2 minutes until it starts to soften. Add the tomatoes and grated apple and cook for 3 minutes until the tomatoes start to soften. Stir in the vinegar and brown sugar, then cover and simmer for 5 minutes, stirring occasionally. Remove from the heat and set aside to cool.

Place a chargrill pan or large frying pan over high heat, add the steaks and cook for 1 minute each side. Transfer to a plate and cover loosely with foil.

Place the lettuce leaves on 4 toast slices, followed by the steaks, avocado and tomato relish. Top with the toasted lids and serve with rainbow chips.

✱ To simplify this recipe, the homemade tomato relish can be swapped for a store-bought relish or replaced with slices of tomato.

Steak sandwich with avocado and tomato relish

Fish and chips with tartare sauce

Fish and chips with tartare sauce
Serves 4

200 g potatoes, scrubbed and cut into 2 cm thick chips
300 g sweet potato, peeled and cut into 2 cm thick chips
olive oil spray
100 g wholemeal plain flour
2 eggs, lightly beaten
1 cup fresh wholemeal breadcrumbs
500 g firm white fish fillets
lemon wedges, to serve

Tartare sauce
½ cup fat-reduced natural yoghurt
1 tablespoon capers in brine, rinsed and finely chopped
2 gherkins, finely chopped
1 tablespoon finely chopped parsley

Preheat the oven to 200°C and line 2 baking trays with baking paper. Place the potato and sweet potato chips on one of the baking trays and lightly spray with olive oil. Bake for 30 minutes until golden and crisp.

Place the flour, eggs and breadcrumbs in 3 separate bowls. Dip the fish in the flour, then in the egg, and finally in the breadcrumbs, shaking off any excess. Place the fish on the second baking tray and lightly spray with olive oil. Bake for the last 10 minutes of the chip cooking time until golden and crisp.

Meanwhile, make the tartare sauce by mixing all the ingredients in a small bowl.

Serve the fish and chips with tartare sauce, lemon wedges and mixed green lettuce leaves.

✱ To simplify this recipe, the homemade tartare sauce can be swapped for a store-bought alternative.

Pork kebabs with chickpea and tomato salad

Pork kebabs with chickpea and tomato salad
Serves 4

8 bamboo skewers

1 teaspoon dried thyme

grated zest and juice of 1 orange

2 teaspoons seeded mustard

2 tablespoons tomato sauce

2 teaspoons honey

500 g pork fillet, cut into 3 cm cubes

2 small red onions, cut into 2 cm cubes

1 yellow capsicum, cut into 2 cm cubes

2 zucchini, cut into 1 cm slices

1 tablespoon olive oil

Chickpea and tomato salad

400 g can chickpeas, drained and rinsed

2 ripe tomatoes, cut into 1 cm dice

1 carrot, cut into 1 cm dice

1 cucumber, halved lengthways, seeded and sliced

2 cups baby spinach leaves

1 tablespoon balsamic vinegar

2 tablespoons olive oil

Soak the bamboo skewers for 15 minutes to prevent them from scorching during the cooking process.

Mix the thyme, orange zest and juice, mustard, tomato sauce and honey in a large bowl. Add the pork and stir until well coated in the marinade. Cover and refrigerate for 15 minutes.

Thread the pork, onion, capsicum and zucchini onto the skewers. Heat the oil in a large frying pan over medium heat and cook the skewers for 6 minutes on each side, turning once, or until cooked through.

To make the salad, combine the chickpeas, tomato, carrot, cucumber and spinach in a large bowl. Drizzle the balsamic vinegar and olive oil over the top and gently toss. Serve the salad in individual dishes alongside the kebabs.

Chicken and zucchini nuggets with corn and pumpkin dip
Serves 4

1 cup wholemeal plain flour
3 eggs, lightly beaten
1½ cups dried multigrain breadcrumbs
2 teaspoons dried mixed herbs
2 zucchini, cut into 6 cm long chips
500 g chicken breast, cut into 3 cm cubes
olive oil spray
garden salad (see page 213), to serve

Corn and pumpkin dip
300 g pumpkin, peeled and roughly chopped
310 g creamed corn

Preheat the oven to 200°C and line a baking tray with baking paper. Place the flour and beaten egg in two separate bowls. Combine the breadcrumbs and herbs in a third bowl. Dip each zucchini chip and chicken piece in the flour, then in the egg, and finally in the breadcrumbs, shaking off any excess. (Doing each piece individually prevents them sticking together.)

Place the chicken and zucchini in a single layer on the baking tray and spray with olive oil. Bake for 10–12 minutes or until golden and crisp, and the chicken is cooked through.

Meanwhile, place the pumpkin in a small saucepan of water, bring to the boil and simmer for 10 minutes or until tender. Drain and return to the saucepan. Mash the pumpkin until smooth, then stir in the creamed corn.

Serve the chicken and zucchini nuggets with the dip and a garden salad.

Sang choy bau
Serves 4

100 g vermicelli (glass) noodles
1 tablespoon canola oil
1 small brown onion, finely diced
1 clove garlic, finely diced
500 g lean minced pork
2 cm piece ginger, peeled and finely grated
handful of button mushrooms, sliced
small handful of green beans,
     trimmed and cut into 1 cm pieces
1 carrot, coarsely grated
1 zucchini, coarsely grated
2 tablespoons hoisin sauce
8 small iceberg lettuce leaves
1 tablespoon sesame seeds, lightly toasted

Soak the vermicelli in cold water for 10 minutes until softened. Drain and roughly chop a quarter of the noodles.

Heat the oil in a large frying pan over medium heat and cook the onion and garlic for 2 minutes or until the onion starts to soften. Add the mince and cook for 5 minutes or until browned. Add the ginger, mushrooms, beans, carrot and zucchini and cook for 2 minutes or until the mushrooms soften. Stir in the hoisin and noodles and cook for 2 minutes until heated through.

Spoon the mixture into the lettuce cups, sprinkle with the sesame seeds and serve.

✱ Omit the sesame seeds if there is a seed allergy in the family.

Sang choy bau

Ham, mushroom and capsicum pita pizzas

Ham, mushroom and capsicum pita pizzas
Makes 4

4 small wholemeal pita breads

140 g pizza tomato paste

1 cup grated pizza cheese

200 g lean sliced ham, finely shredded

150 g mushrooms, finely sliced

1 red capsicum, seeded and finely sliced

2 teaspoons dried oregano

garden salad (see page 213),
    or chickpea and tomato salad
    (see page 245), to serve

Preheat the oven to 200°C and line 2 baking trays with baking paper. Place the pita breads on the trays and spread each evenly with the pizza paste. Top with cheese, ham, mushroom, capsicum and oregano. Bake for 15 minutes, or until the cheese is melted and golden and the base is crisp. Cut into quarters and serve immediately with a garden salad or chickpea and tomato salad.

✱ Slices of pizza make a great lunchbox addition.

✱ Pizza cheese is a mixture of mozzarella, cheddar and parmesan. It is available in most supermarkets, but if you can't find it use grated fat-reduced mozzarella or cheddar instead.

Variations
Barbecue chicken and tomato pita pizzas
Among the 4 pita breads, divide 1 cup grated pizza cheese, 500 g shredded roast chicken, 1 small red onion, finely chopped, and ½ punnet of cherry tomatoes, each tomato halved. Drizzle each pizza with ½ teaspoon barbecue sauce and bake as in the basic recipe.

Mexican beef and mushroom pita pizzas
Among the 4 pita breads, divide 1 cup grated fat-reduced cheese, 500 g sliced roast beef, 2 cups sliced mushrooms and ⅔ cup tomato salsa. Sprinkle a small pinch of ground cumin over each. Bake as in the basic recipe.

Tomato and baby bocconcini pizzas
Among the 4 pita breads, divide 1 cup fat-reduced cheddar cheese, 2 tomatoes, finely diced, 2 tablespoons chopped basil leaves and 8 baby bocconcini, each one halved. Bake as in the basic recipe.

Fishcakes with green salad and pesto mayonnaise

Serve 4

400 g potatoes, cut into quarters
150 g frozen peas
400 g can salmon, drained and mashed
¼ cup roughly chopped parsley
grated zest and juice of 1 lemon
80 g dried multigrain breadcrumbs
2 tablespoons olive oil

Green salad and pesto mayonnaise
½ cup fat-reduced mayonnaise
2 tablespoons pesto
2 cups rocket
1 pear, sliced
1 zucchini, grated

Preheat the oven to 200°C and line a baking tray with baking paper. Place the potato in a saucepan of cold water, bring to the boil over high heat and cook for 8–10 minutes or until just tender. Add the peas and cook for a further minute. Drain, then return the potato and peas to the pan and mash. Set aside to cool.

Mix the salmon, parsley, lemon zest and juice and pea mash in a large bowl. Roll into 8 balls, then cover and refrigerate for 30 minutes. Roll lightly in the breadcrumbs to coat, and flatten slightly.

Heat the oil in a large frying pan and gently fry half the fishcakes for 2 minutes each side in order to brown them. Transfer to the baking tray and repeat with the remaining fishcakes. Bake for 10 minutes until crisp and heated through.

Combine the mayonnaise, pesto and 1 tablespoon warm water in a small bowl. Place the rocket, pear and zucchini in a salad bowl and toss to combine. Serve the fishcakes with the rocket salad and pesto mayonnaise.

✱ These fishcakes freeze well for up to a month.

Beef and vegetable pastries
Makes 4

1 tablespoon canola oil

1 onion, finely diced

500 g lean minced beef (or lean minced chicken or pork)

2 tablespoons salt-reduced tomato sauce

2 teaspoons curry powder (optional)

1 cup salt-reduced beef stock

200 g pumpkin, peeled and cut into 1 cm cubes

1 cup mixed frozen vegetables

1 cup frozen peas

8 sheets filo pastry

olive oil spray

vegie slaw (see page 213), to serve

Preheat the oven to 200°C and line a baking tray with baking paper. Heat the oil in a large frying pan over medium heat and cook the onion for 2 minutes until it starts to soften. Add the mince and cook for 5 minutes until browned. Stir in the tomato sauce, curry powder, stock and pumpkin and simmer for 10 minutes until the pumpkin is soft and the stock has evaporated. Add the vegetables and peas, mix well, then set aside to cool.

Spray one sheet of filo with olive oil, then top with a second sheet. Fold the pastry in half (short side to short side) and place 1 cup of the beef mixture on the short side of the folded pastry. Fold the pastry over the filling, then tuck in the sides and roll up to enclose. Place seam-side down on the baking tray. Repeat with the remaining filo and filling to make 4 pastries. Bake for 20 minutes until golden and crisp, then serve with vegie slaw.

✱ You can use leftover roast vegetables in place of the vegies in this recipe.

Variation
Lunchbox-sized pastries
To make handy lunchbox alternatives to sandwiches, make 8 smaller pastries. For each pastry, use 1 sheet of filo and ½ cup of filling. Bake for 10–15 minutes until golden and crisp.

Corn and pea fritters
(page 145)

Tandoori chicken skewers (page 223)

bring-a-plate ideas

Many of the recipes in this book are suitable for taking to kid-friendly parties or get-togethers. Try some of the ones featured here.

Grilled fruit swords (page 256)

Apple muffins (page 263)

Chicken and zucchini nuggets with corn and pumpkin dip (page 246)

something
sweet

Magic wands with berry yoghurt
Makes 4

8 strawberries
1 mango, peeled and cut into 2 cm chunks
2 kiwi fruit, peeled and quartered
2 small peaches, quartered
1 small star fruit, cut into 1 cm slices
4 long bamboo skewers
400 g fat-reduced berry yoghurt

Thread a strawberry and a piece of mango, kiwi fruit, peach and star fruit onto each skewer, then repeat, finishing with a star fruit top. Serve with the yoghurt for dipping.

Strawberry and banana popsicles
Makes 6

400 g fat-reduced strawberry yoghurt
100 g strawberries, hulled and quartered
1 small banana, peeled and roughly chopped

Place all the ingredients in a blender and whiz until smooth. Spoon into six 100 ml popsicle moulds with lids, then freeze for 4 hours or overnight until set.

✱ If you don't own popsicle moulds, pour the mixture into 4 small plastic cups. Place a clean popsicle stick in each cup and freeze for 4 hours or overnight until set.

Grilled fruit swords
Makes 4

4 long bamboo skewers
300 g pineapple, peeled and cut into
    8 even-sized chunks
1 large banana, peeled and cut into
    8 even-sized rounds
1 pear, peeled and cut into 8 even-sized
    chunks
1 tablespoon honey
1 teaspoon margarine
400 g fat-reduced vanilla yoghurt

Soak the bamboo skewers for 15 minutes to prevent them from scorching during the cooking process.

Preheat the grill to hot. Thread a piece of pineapple, banana and pear onto each skewer, then repeat. Place the skewers on a baking tray.

Melt the honey and margarine in a small saucepan, then brush over the fruit. Grill for 3 minutes, then turn over and grill for a further 3 minutes until golden. Set aside for 5 minutes to cool, then serve with yoghurt for dipping.

Magic wands with berry yoghurt

Strawberry and banana popsicles

Apple and blueberry crumble
Serves 4

1 quantity of cinnamon apple (see page 138) or
    400 g can apple pie fruit
200 g frozen blueberries
½ cup wholemeal plain flour
1 tablespoon brown sugar
¾ cup rolled oats
1 tablespoon margarine
fat-reduced vanilla yoghurt, to serve

Preheat the oven to 200°C. Place the apples and blueberries in a large bowl and gently mix. Spoon into a 1.5-litre ceramic ovenproof dish.

Place the flour, sugar and oats in a bowl. Using your fingertips, rub the margarine into the dry ingredients until well combined. Spoon the mixture over the fruit and bake for 20 minutes until golden. Serve with vanilla yoghurt.

✷ In place of the blueberries you could use any seasonal fruit. Try apricots, peaches, raspberries or strawberries.

Apple and rhubarb strudel
Serves 8

1 quantity of cinnamon apple (see page 138)
1 quantity of ruby red rhubarb (see page 138)
4 sheets filo pastry
canola oil spray

Preheat the oven to 180°C and line a baking tray with baking paper. Combine the cinnamon apples and stewed rhubarb in a bowl.

Lay out one sheet of filo pastry on the bench, lightly spray with canola oil and top with another sheet of filo. Spray again and repeat with the remaining sheets of filo, finishing with a light spray of oil. Spread the fruit mixture lengthways along the centre of the pastry, leaving a 5 cm gap at each end. Fold in the two short sides, then roll up the strudel to form a long roll. Place on the baking tray, seam-side down, and bake for 20 minutes or until the pastry is crisp and golden.

Apple and rhubarb strudel

Orange and vanilla poached pears
Serves 4

2 teaspoons vanilla extract
1 stick cinnamon
1 cup orange juice
2 tablespoons brown sugar
4 small pears, peeled, cored and quartered
1 cup fat-reduced custard
2 tablespoons flaked almonds, lightly toasted

Place the vanilla, cinnamon, orange juice, sugar and 2 cups water in a saucepan over medium heat. Bring to the boil, then reduce the heat and simmer for 5 minutes.

Add the pears and simmer for a further 5 minutes or until the pears have softened, then remove the pan from the heat. Cover and set aside for 15 minutes.

Divide the pears among 4 serving dishes. Serve with a dollop of custard, sprinkled with almonds.

✻ Omit the almonds if there is a nut allergy in the family.

Fruit scones
Makes 12

¾ cup wholemeal self-raising flour, plus extra for dusting
1 tablespoon brown sugar
25 g margarine
1 cup dried fruit (such as currants, sultanas or pitted prunes)
½ cup fat-reduced milk
½ teaspoon white vinegar

Preheat the oven to 220°C. Place the flour and sugar in a food processor, add the margarine and pulse until the mixture resembles breadcrumbs. Add the fruit, milk and vinegar and pulse until just combined. Alternatively, place the flour, sugar and margarine into a large mixing bowl. Using your fingertips, rub the margarine into the flour and sugar until the mixture resembles breadcrumbs. Add the fruit, milk and vinegar and stir until just combined.

✻ Turn out the dough onto a lightly floured surface and gently press out with your fingers to a thickness of about 3 cm.

✻ Lightly flour a 20 cm cake tin. Dip a 5 cm round cutter in flour and cut scones from the dough. Place the scones in the cake tin (side by side) and sprinkle with a little extra flour. Bake for 12–15 minutes until golden.

✻ These are also great as lunchbox snacks.

Baked vanilla custard
Serves 4

2 cups fat-reduced milk
3 eggs
2 teaspoons vanilla extract
2 tablespoons caster sugar
¼ teaspoon ground cinnamon
¼ teaspoon ground nutmeg

Preheat the oven to 160°C. Place the milk in a small saucepan over medium heat and heat until hot (do not allow to boil). Set aside.

Place the eggs, vanilla, sugar, cinnamon and nutmeg in a large heatproof bowl and whisk until combined. Slowly pour the hot milk into the egg mixture, whisking constantly until smooth and combined. Pour the custard into four ¾-cup ramekins.

Place the ramekins in a deep baking dish and pour enough boiling water into the dish to come halfway up the sides of the ramekins. Transfer the dish to the oven and bake for 40 minutes or until just set. Remove from the oven and allow to cool slightly. Serve warm.

Variation
Baked fruit custard
Spoon 1 cup sliced, drained canned peaches, pears or apricots into the base of a 1.5 litre ceramic dish. Pour the uncooked custard over the top and bake for 1 hour or until just set.

Stirred vanilla custard
Serves 4

2 cups fat-reduced milk
1 teaspoon vanilla extract
4 egg yolks
2 tablespoons caster sugar
1 tablespoon cornflour

Place the milk and vanilla in a small saucepan over medium heat and heat until hot (do not allow to boil). Set aside.

Place the egg yolks, sugar and cornflour in a large bowl and whisk until smooth. Slowly pour the hot milk into the egg mixture, whisking constantly until smooth and combined. Pour the custard into a clean saucepan and cook over low heat for 10 minutes, stirring constantly until the custard thickens and coats the back of a spoon (it should be the same consistency as thickened cream). Serve warm or cold.

* If you prefer a thicker custard, add an extra teaspoon of cornflour.

Variation
Chocolate custard
Add 2 tablespoons cocoa powder to the mixture when you add the cornflour, and continue with the recipe above.

Orange sultana muffins

Orange sultana muffins
Makes 12

125 g wholemeal self-raising flour
125 g self-raising flour
½ cup caster sugar
¼ cup sultanas
2 eggs, lightly beaten
¼ cup extra-light olive oil
250 ml fat-reduced milk
1 teaspoon vanilla extract
grated zest and juice of 2 oranges

Preheat the oven to 200°C and line 12 × ⅓ cup muffin holes with paper cases. Place the flours, sugar and sultanas in a large mixing bowl and stir to combine. Place the beaten egg, oil, milk and vanilla in a small jug and lightly whisk with a fork. Add to the dry ingredients and mix with a large metal spoon until just incorporated. Stir in the orange zest and juice.

Spoon the batter into the paper cases and bake for 20 minutes or until the muffins are golden and spring back when lightly touched.

Apple muffins
Omit the sultanas from the basic recipe and replace the orange zest and juice with 1 Granny Smith apple, cut into ½ cm cubes. Add ½ teaspoon mixed spice to the mixture. Bake as in the basic recipe.

Banana muffins
Omit the sultanas from the basic recipe and replace the orange zest and juice with 1 ripe banana, mashed. Add ¼ teaspoon ground nutmeg to the mixture. Bake as in the basic recipe.

Chocolate and pear muffins
Replace the sultanas from the basic recipe with 2 teaspoons cocoa powder. Replace the orange zest and juice with 1 ripe pear, cut into ½ cm cubes. Bake as in the basic recipe.

Vanilla strawberry celebration sponge cake
Serves 12

canola oil spray
$\frac{1}{3}$ cup wholemeal self-raising flour
$\frac{1}{3}$ cup white self-raising flour
$\frac{1}{3}$ cup cornflour
$\frac{1}{4}$ cup caster sugar
4 eggs
2 teaspoons vanilla extract
120 g smooth fat-reduced ricotta
1 tablespoon icing sugar, plus extra for dusting
250 g strawberries, hulled and chopped

Preheat the oven to 160°C. Spray 2 × 20 cm round cake tins with canola oil and line the base and sides with baking paper. Line a wire cake rack with baking paper.

Sift the flours three times into a bowl (this will help aerate the cake, making it lighter).

Whisk the sugar, eggs and vanilla in an electric mixer for 10 minutes until pale and thick and doubled in size. Fold in the flours with a large metal spoon until just mixed.

Spoon the batter into the prepared tins, dividing evenly between the 2 tins. Bake for 20 minutes until the cakes are golden and spring back when lightly touched. Cool on the wire rack.

Place one cake on a serving plate or stand. Combine the ricotta and icing sugar in a bowl, then fold in the strawberries. Spread the ricotta mixture over the cake and top with the remaining sponge. Dust with icing sugar and serve.

✱ This recipe is great when you are looking for a healthier alternative for celebrations or special occasions.

Vanilla strawberry celebration sponge cake

BMI chart: girls (2 to 20 years)

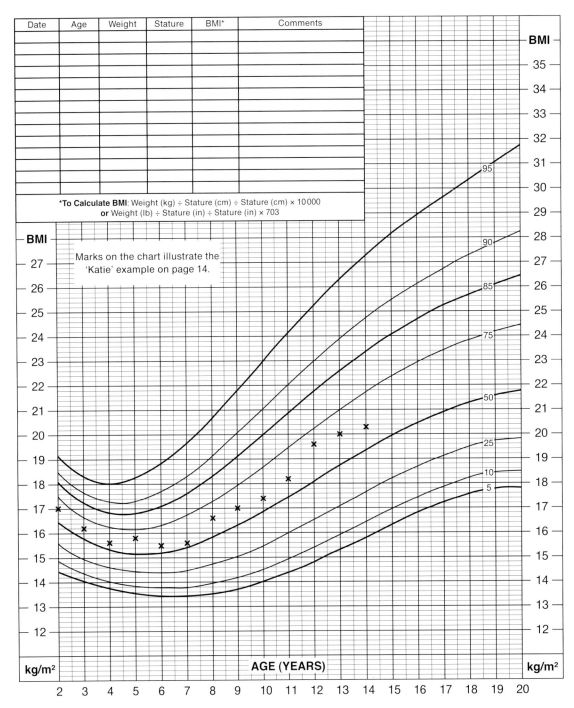

Date	Age	Weight	Stature	BMI*	Comments

*To Calculate BMI: Weight (kg) ÷ Stature (cm) ÷ Stature (cm) × 10 000
or Weight (lb) ÷ Stature (in) ÷ Stature (in) × 703

BMI

Marks on the chart illustrate the 'Katie' example on page 14.

AGE (YEARS)

kg/m²

SOURCE: Developed by the National Center for Health Statistics in collaboration with
the National Center for Chronic Disease Prevention ad Health Promotion (2000),
http://www.cdc.gov/growthcharts

BMI chart: boys (2 to 20 years)

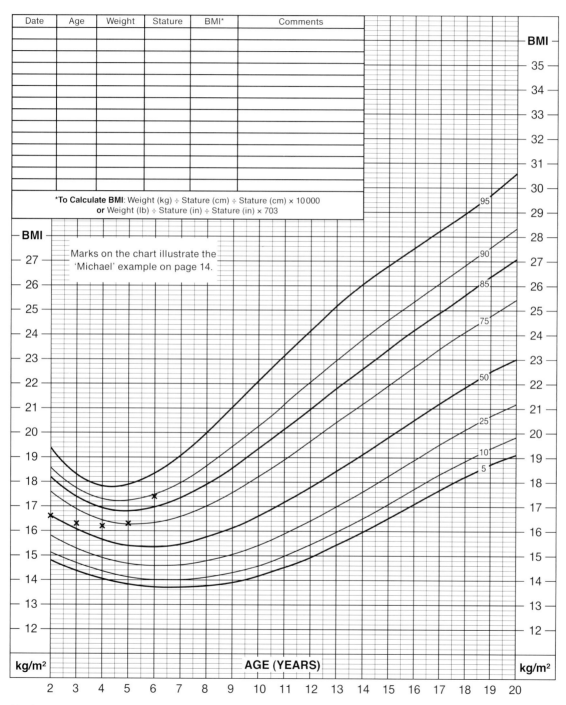

Date	Age	Weight	Stature	BMI*	Comments

*To Calculate BMI: Weight (kg) ÷ Stature (cm) ÷ Stature (cm) × 10000
or Weight (lb) ÷ Stature (in) ÷ Stature (in) × 703

Marks on the chart illustrate the 'Michael' example on page 14.

BMI

AGE (YEARS)

kg/m²

kg/m²

SOURCE: Developed by the National Center for Health Statistics in collaboration with
the National Center for Chronic Disease Prevention ad Health Promotion (2000),
http://www.cdc.gov/growthcharts

References

American Academy of Pediatrics Committee on Public Education. Children, adolescents, and television. *Pediatrics* 2001; 107(2): 423–6.

Australian Communications and Media Authority, *Media and Communications in Australian Families 2007: Report of the Media and Society Research Project*, Canberra, December 2007.

Barton, B.A., Eldridge, A.L., Thompson, D., Affenito, S.G., Striegel-Moore, R.H., Franko, D.L., Albertson, A.M. & Crockett, S.J. The relationship of breakfast and cereal consumption to nutrient intake and body mass index: the National Heart, Lung, and Blood Institute Growth and Health Study. *Journal of the American Dietetic Association* 2005; 105(9): 1383–9.

Bauer, K.W., Nelson, M.C., Boutelle, K.N. & Neumark-Sztainer, D. Parental influences on adolescents' physical activity and sedentary behaviour: longitudinal findings from Project EAT-II. *International Journal of Behavioral Nutrition and Physical Activity* 2008; 5:12.

Bell, A.C. & Swinburn, B.A. What are the key food groups to target for preventing obesity and improving nutrition in schools? *European Journal of Clinical Nutrition* 2004; 58(2): 258–63.

Buijzen, M., Schuurman, J. & Bomhof, E. Associations between children's television advertising exposure and their food consumption patterns: a household diary – survey study. *Appetite* 2008; 50(2–3): 231–9.

Campbell, K., Crawford, D. & Ball, K. Family food environment and dietary behaviors likely to promote fatness in 5–6 year-old children. *International Journal of Obesity* 2006; 30: 1272–80.

Campbell, K., Hesketh, K., Crawford, D., Salmon, J., Ball, K. & McCallum, Z. The Infant Feeding Activity and Nutrition Trial (INFANT) an early intervention to prevent childhood obesity: cluster-randomised controlled trial. *BMC Public Health* 2008; 8: 103.

Capaldi, E.D. & Privitera, G.J. Decreasing dislike for sour and bitter in children and adults. *Appetite* 2008; 50(1): 139–45.

Chau, J. & Farrell, L. *Building Solutions for Preventing Childhood Obesity. Module 5: Interventions to increase physical activity in children between five and twelve years of age.* NSW Centre for Overweight and Obesity, Sydney, 2008.

Cooke, L. The importance of exposure for healthy eating in childhood: a review. *Journal of Human Nutrition and Dietetics* 2007; 20(4): 294–301.

Davison, K.K. & Campbell, K. Opportunities to prevent obesity in children within families: an ecological approach, chapter 10 in Crawford, D. & Jeffery, R.W. (eds.), *Obesity Prevention and Public Health*, Oxford University Press, Oxford, 2005.

Delmas, C., Platat, C., Schweitzer, B., Wagner, A., Oujaa, M. & Simon, C. Association between television in bedroom and adiposity throughout adolescence. *Obesity* 2007; 15(10): 2495–503.

Department of Health and Ageing, *Active Kids are Healthy Kids: Australia's Physical Activity Recommendations for 5–12 year olds*, Canberra, 2004.

Department of Health and Ageing, *Get out and Get Active: Australia's Physical Activity Recommendations for 12–18 year olds*, Canberra, 2004.

Department of Health and Ageing, *Draft national physical activity recommendations for children 0–5**, Canberra, 2008. (*These recommendations are draft and subject to endorsement by the Australian Health Minister.)

Dovey, T.M., Staples, P.A., Gibson, E.L. & Halford, J.C.G. Food neophobia and 'picky/fussy' eating in children: a review. *Appetite* 2008; 50(2–3): 181–93.

Farrell, L. & Chau, J. *Building Solutions for Preventing Childhood Obesity. Module 6: Interventions to increase physical activity in adolescents.* NSW Centre for Overweight and Obesity, Sydney, 2008.

Farrell, L., Hardy, L. & Torvaldsen, S. *Building Solutions for Preventing Childhood Obesity. Module 7: Interventions to reduce sedentary behaviours.* NSW Centre for Overweight and Obesity, Sydney, 2008.

Gunner, K.B., Atkinson, P.M., Nichols, J. & Eissa, M.A. Health promotion strategies to encourage physical activity in infants, toddlers, and preschoolers. *Journal of Pediatric Health Care* 2005; 19(4): 253–8.

Hardy, L., Bass, S. & Booth, M. Changes in sedentary behavior among adolescent girls: a 2.5-year prospective cohort study. *Journal of Adolescent Health* 2007; 40(2): 158–65.

Hardy, L., Baur, L., Garnett, S., Crawford, D., Campbell, K., Shrewsbury, V., Cowell, C. & Salmon, J. Family and home correlates of television viewing in 12–13 year old adolescents: the Nepean Study. *International Journal of Behavioral Nutrition and Physical Activity* 2006; 3: 24.

Hardy, L., Dobbins, T., Denney-Wilson, E., Okely, A. & Booth, M. Descriptive epidemiology of small screen recreation among Australian adolescents. *Journal of Paediatrics and Child Health* 2006; 42(11): 709–14.

Hattersley, L. & Hector, D. *Building Solutions for Preventing Childhood Obesity. Module 1. Interventions to promote consumption of water and reduce consumption of sugary drinks.* NSW Centre for Overweight and Obesity, Sydney, 2008.

Havermans, R.C. & Jansen, A. Increasing children's liking of vegetables through flavour-flavour learning. *Appetite* 2007; 48(2): 259–62.

Hector, D. & Hattersley, L. *Building Solutions for Preventing Childhood Obesity. Module 4: Interventions to promote eating breakfast.* NSW Centre for Overweight and Obesity, Sydney, 2008.

Huntley, R. *Because Family Mealtimes Matter.* White Paper. Ipsos Australia, 2008.

Iglowstein, I., Jenni, O.G., Molinari, L. & Largo, R.H. Sleep duration from infancy to adolescence: reference values and generational trends. *Pediatrics* 2003; 111(2): 302–7.

Ipsos-Eureka Social Research Institute. (2007, December). Research to Inform the Wellbeing Plan for Children (Ipsos Public Affairs Project 4131). Sydney, Australia.

Mennella, J.A., Nicklaus, S., Jagolino, A.L. & Yourshaw, L.M. Variety is the spice of life: strategies for promoting fruit and vegetable acceptance during infancy. *Physiology & Behavior* 2008; 94(1): 29–38.

Moore, M. & Meltzer, L.J. The sleepy adolescent: causes and consequences of sleepiness in teens. *Paediatric Respiratory Reviews* 2008; 9(2): 114–21.

Morgenthaler, T.I., Owens, J., Alessi, C., Boehlecke, B., Brown, T.M., Coleman, J., Friedman, L., Kapur V.K., Lee-Chiong, T., Pancer, J. & Swick, T.J. Practice parameters for behavioral treatment of bedtime problems and night wakings in infants and young children. *Sleep* 2006; 29(10), 1277–81.

National Association for Sport and Physical Education, *Active Start: A Statement of Physical Activity Guidelines for Children Birth to Five Years*, American Alliance for Health, Physical Education, Recreation and Dance, Reston, VA, 2002.

National Health and Medical Research Council, *Clinical Practice Guidelines for the Management of Overweight and Obesity in Children and Adolescents*, Canberra, 2003.

National Health and Medical Research Council, *Dietary Guidelines for Children and Adolescents in Australia*, Canberra, 2003.

Nixon, G.M., Thompson, J.M., Han, D.Y., Becroft, D.M., Clark, P.M., Robinson, E., Waldie, K.E., Wild, C.J., Black, P.N. & Mitchell, E.A. Short sleep duration in middle childhood: risk factors and consequences. *Sleep* 2008; 31(1): 71–8.

O'Dea, J.A. Why do kids eat healthful food? Perceived benefits of and barriers to healthful eating and physical activity among children and adolescents. *Journal of the American Dietetic Association* 2003; 103(4): 497–501.

Owens J., Maxim R., McGuinn M., Nobile C., Msall M. & Alario A. Television-viewing habits and sleep disturbances in school children. *Pediatrics* 1999; 104(3):e27.

Pliner, P. Cognitive schemas: how can we use them to improve children's acceptance of diverse and unfamiliar foods? *British Journal of Nutrition* 2008; 99 Suppl 1: S2–6.

Salmon, J., Hume, C., Ball, K., Booth, M. & Crawford, D. Individual, social and home environment determinants of change in children's television viewing: the Switch-Play intervention. *Journal of Science and Medicine in Sport* 2006; 9(5): 378–87.

Sanigorski, A.M., Bell, A.C., Kremer, P.J. & Swinburn, B.A. Lunchbox contents of Australian school children: room for improvement. *European Journal of Clinical Nutrition* 2005; 59(11): 1310–6.

Shriver, E.K. National Institute of Child Health and Human Development, *Adventures in Parenting (00-4842)*, Washington, DC, U.S. Government Printing Office, 2001.

Spurrier, N.J., Magarey, A.A., Golley, R.K., Curnow, F. & Sawyer, M.G. Relationships between the home environment and physical activity and dietary patterns in preschool children: a cross-sectional study. *International Journal of Behavioral Nutrition and Physical Activity* 2008; 5:31.

Van Zutphen M., Bell, A.C., Kremer, P.J. & Swinburn, B.A. Association between the family environment and television viewing in Australian children. *Journal of Paediatrics and Child Health* 2007; 43(6): 458–63.

Ventura, A.K. & Birch, L.L. Does parenting affect children's eating and weight status? *International Journal of Behavioral Nutrition and Physical Activity* 2008; 5:15.

Wardle, J., Cooke, L.J., Gibson, E.L., Sapochnik, M., Sheiham, A. & Lawson, M. Increasing children's acceptance of vegetables; a randomized trial of parent-led exposure. *Appetite* 2003; 40(2): 155–62.

Wardle, J., Herrera, M.L., Cooke, L. & Gibson, E.L. Modifying children's food preferences: the effects of exposure and reward on acceptance of an unfamiliar vegetable. *European Journal of Clinical Nutrition* 2003; 57(2): 341–48.

Watson, D.L. & Tharp, R.G. *Self-directed Behavior: Self-modification for Personal Adjustment*, 9th edn. Wadsworth/Thomson Learning, Belmont, CA, 2007.

See also:

Australasian Society of Clinical Immunology and Allergy: Position papers, guidelines, recommendations and advice, located at allergy.org.au

Body Mass Index-for-age Percentile Charts. Developed by the National Centre for Health Statistics in collaboration with the National Centre for Chronic Disease Prevention and Health Promotion (2000.) http://www.cdc.gov/growthcharts

Index